NATURE
CRAFTS

NATURE CRAFTS

CRAFTS

Anne Orth Epple

Chilton Book Company
Radnor, Pennsylvania

Copyright © 1974 by Anne Orth Epple
First Edition   *All Rights Reserved*
Second Printing, May 1975

Published in Radnor, Pa., by Chilton Book Company
and simultaneously in Don Mills, Ontario, Canada,
by Thomas Nelson & Sons, Ltd.

Photographs by Lewis E. Epple
Designed by Cypher Associates, Inc.

Manufactured in the United States of America

Library of Congress Cataloging in Publication Data
Epple, Anne Orth.
   Nature crafts.
   (Creative crafts series)
   1. Handicraft. I. Title.
TT157.E66   745.5   73-20367
ISBN 0-8019-5939-X
ISBN 0-8019-5940-3 (pbk.)

*To my husband, Lew,
whose help and encouragement
made this book possible.*

CONTENTS

AUTHOR'S NOTES

My collecting instinct led to the creation of this book—a book of ideas to help you, too, create inexpensive designs using nature's collectibles. And so, while your friends are frantically searching through department stores and novelty shops for unusual gifts and home accessories, you will be creating your own. Each creation will be original and when asked, "Where did you ever buy such a lovely . . .?" you will answer with pride, "I made it."

I hope that this book will spark your imagination and that you will use my designs as springboards to your own creativity. Start by collecting the ingredients which nature supplies. Next, prepare your materials and store them as suggested in this text, since the durability of the finished design depends entirely on the proper preparation of your basic materials.

Nature's collectibles can be found everywhere: fields, gardens, deserts, beaches, mountains and even city parks. In many instances, you can use artificial materials in place of natural ones. In this way, you copy nature without collecting rare or protected plants and help preserve nature for future generations to enjoy.

NATURE CRAFTS

Chapter *1*
The Home
Workshop

Think big or think small! The size of your workshop is entirely your decision. Choose from the space you have available, but consider convenience of location more vital than spaciousness. For example, my workshop consists of a long, sturdy table located in one corner of our family room—convenient to the kitchen, the phone and the door.

Every workshop, regardless of size, needs a sturdy table (naturally the larger, the better), good lighting and certain basic supplies. For your convenience in setting up your workshop, I have compiled four separate lists of supplies and materials.

NATURE'S COLLECTIBLES

List 1 consists of nature's collectibles, which are everywhere. These are some of the common items to collect for use in your nature designs:

Bark	Fruits	Pebbles
Berries	Fungus	Pits
Birds' nests (empty)	Gemstones	Plant materials
Butterflies (dead)	Glass, weathered	Pods
Cones	Leaves	Rocks
Cork	Lichens	Sand
Decorative wood	Mosses	Sea life
Feathers	Moths (dead)	Seeds
Fern fronds	Mushrooms	Shells
Flowers	Nuts	Vine tendrils

Collect these treasures in moderation, always keeping in mind the fact that nothing in nature is endless, especially if wasted or abused. Collect only in areas where it is permissible to gather these natural materials, never on private lands or in state or national parks. Know the conservation laws of your state before picking flowers or foliage.

When gathering plant materials, cut off the leaves or flowers with sharp scissors or shears, so as not to tear the stems of the plants and, also, to leave their roots undisturbed. When collecting cones, pods or dried-in-the-field materials, shake all the seeds free, whenever possible, before bringing the materials home. (I do a great deal of my collecting in areas where the land is being cleared for roads or building construction.)

MISCELLANEOUS SUPPLIES

List 2 consists of miscellaneous bits and scraps to save for use in your natural creations. Don't buy any of the things mentioned on List 2; save a small supply of each. Store these things in labeled boxes near your worktable so that they are handy when you need them.

Baskets   For dried arrangement containers.

Books, pocket-sized   For pressing plants in the field.

Bottle caps (screw-on-type)   For miniature plant containers.

Broomsticks   For "tree" trunks.

Brown paper bags   For collecting, drying and storing.

Brown wrapping paper   For making stationery and fake fur outline.

Butterfly and moth pictures   For use in making pictures.

Cake tins with covers   For desiccants and for storage.

Can, ham, coffee, shortening and others   Many uses.

Candle stubs   For sealing sand parfait designs.

Cardboard of various weights   Numerous uses.

Cardboard boxes of different sizes   Many uses.

Corsage pins or hat pins   For reuse on corsages.

Dishes, porcelain or china   For gluing, cementing, inking.

Drawer pulls, wooden   For miniature plant containers.

Eggshells, blown   For Easter designs.

Flowerpots   Plant containers for topiaries.

Glass   For use with ink and a brayer.

Gloves, old   To wear when working with evergreens or wire.

Jars with covers   For storing desiccant-dried plants.

Leg cups from furniture   Miniature plant containers.

Magazines   For pressing plant materials in newspapers.

Molding   For framing pictures. (Get scraps at building sites.)

Newspapers   Many uses.

Picture frames   For reuse in pressed flower pictures.

Plastic containers   For mixing glue, cement, paint and sand.

Plastic covers from Cool Whip® and large cans   For small plaques.

Postal and greeting card pictures   Pictures for framing.

Rags   Many uses.

Rubber inner tubes   For making rubber animal tracks.

Sheeting   For winding wreaths or trying ink prints.

Shirt buttons   For eyes.

Spray can tops   To use (weighted) upside-down for candles.

Sticks, clean wooden   For stirring paint and plaster.

Teaspoons and tablespoons   For pouring sand and mixing.

Telephone books   For pressing plant materials.

Threads of all colors   For sewing and making insect feelers.

Toothbrushes   For cleaning cones, plaster casts and making spatter prints.

Wire coat hangers   For wreath and mobile frames.

Wood of all kinds and sizes   Check building sites and get permission to collect scrap wood and molding. Endless uses.

Wool   For tiny scarfs and flower centers.

BASIC EQUIPMENT AND TOOLS

List 3 consists of basic equipment and tools which are needed for the numerous projects in this book. To start, look around your home and gather up as many of the materials on this list as possible. Place equipment and tools in a shallow cardboard box on or near your worktable.

Acrylic, clear spray   Endless uses.

Awl or ice pick

Brushes (various size paintbrushes)   Small ones for applying glue; larger ones for painting. Scrub brush for preparing materials. Soft artist's brush for dusting.

Clothespins (snap)   For applying pressure to gluing parts.

Cord   For hanging and tying.

Drill, hand (with different sized drills)   Many uses.

Duco Cement®   A must!

Elmer's Glue-All®   Another must!

Gr·r·rip®   Can be used in place of Elmer's Glue-All.

Hammer

Insect spray   For spraying flowers, wood and nests.

Knapsack   For collecting.

Knife   Keep it sharp.

Modeling clay, green and also brown   For affixing plant materials to containers and for forming molds.

Mothballs   For insect-proofing dried plant materials.

Nails of various sizes

Needles and straight pins

Notebook   For recording your own areas for collecting and the best times to gather nature's collectibles.

Nylon fishing line or dental floss   For making jewelry and mobiles.

Paints, shellac, varnish or stains   Spray cans or regular cans for covering large surfaces. Small bottles of model enamels for touchups and adding dabs of color.

Paper, construction   Various colors, including black.

Paper clips

Paper towels

Pencils, lead and colored pencils

Pens, black and other colored, waterproof felt-tipped   For drawing faces and designs.

Pipe cleaners   For arms and legs and for attaching materials.

Pliers, long-nosed   Many uses.

Pruning shears   For cutting branches and evergreens.

Razor blades, single-edged   For cutting cardboard, Styrofoam® and removing shell flowers.

Rubber bands

Ruler or tape measure

Sandpaper of different grades   For sanding wood, plaster of Paris and cut plant materials.

Saws, hand and coping and keyhole

Scissors

Screws of various sizes and also screw eyes

Stickum®, green and also white   For affixing materials.

Tin snips   For cutting metal or inner tubes.

Toothpicks   For adding dabs of glue, cement or paint.

Tweezers, regular size and long   Many uses.

Vaseline®   Used when making animal tracks and shell flowers.

Wire   Size 20 or 22 and size 24 or 26 wire for wiring dried materials. A spool of fine copper wire for tiny materials. Medium weight wire for wreaths and mobiles. Picture wire for hanging pictures and plaques.

Wire cutters   For cutting wire for wreaths and mobiles.

EQUIPMENT FOR SPECIAL PROJECTS

List 4 consists of equipment needed for special projects. Purchase these materials if and when you have a need for them.

Accessories   Artificial animals to add to creations; available at craft, gift and floral shops.

Aluminum or plastic screening   For making a drying rack; available at hardware stores and lumberyards.

Artificial flowers and foliage   Available at dime, floral and other shops.

Artificial spray snow   To spray on winter designs and to top sand parfaits; available at dime and floral shops.

Brayer   For making ink prints; available at craft shops.

Candleholders   Available at floral, craft and dime stores.

Chicken wire   For designing festoons; available at hardware stores.

Disinfectant such as liquid or spray Lysol®   For preparing fungus, gourds and other things; available at grocery stores.

Dowels   Various sizes for topiaries; available at hardware stores and lumberyards.

Epoxy Cement®, clear-drying   For cement jobs where extra strength is needed; available at hardware and dime stores.

Fake fur and felt squares   Available at fabric departments or shops.

Flexible wires   For table mobiles; available at craft shops.

Floral wire and tape   For wiring and taping dried materials; available at craft and floral shops.

Gem polishing equipment   Rock tumbler with grits and polish; available at craft shops and lapidary stores.

Glass terrariums, apothecary jars, parfait and champagne glasses   For several projects; available at dime, department stores and florists.

Glycerin   For preserving foliage; available at drug stores.

Gold chain, braid and cord   For hanging designs; available at craft, floral and fabric stores.

Hardware cloth (1/4 inch)   A heavy wire screening with 1/4 inch square openings used as a framework for open designs; available at hardware stores and lumberyards.

Inked stamp pads   For use with rubber footprints or leaves; available at stationery or dime stores.

Inks, colored   For dyeing sand. (Food coloring fades so use ink instead.) Available at stationery and dime stores.

Jewelry equipment   Jeweler's pliers, jewelry cement, jewelry-making supplies; available at craft and lapidary shops.

Kwik Kover® or Contac®   For making stationery and place mats; available at dime stores.

Lamp equipment   Socket, threaded pipe, wiring and Epoxy Filler Cement®; available at hardware stores.

Leather strips and fancy cord   For pendants; available at craft stores.

Paints (special ones)   For particular designs; available at art shops.

Plaster of Paris   For topiaries, footprints and casts; available at hardware stores.

Plastic eyes   Available at craft shops.

Plastic pail   For cleaning rocks and mixing plaster.

Rattan frames   Available at floral, craft and dime stores.

Ribbon   Various widths and colors for swags, corsages and wreaths; available at fabric and dime stores.

Rock hounding equipment   Rock pick with a square hammer on one end and a sharp point on the other, for breaking up rocks into smaller pieces. Safety glasses for protecting the eyes from flying rock chips. (If you like, add a cold chisel, small shovel and sledgehammer.) Available at hardware stores.

Rope   For making garlands; available at dime and hardware stores.

Silica gel   For drying plant materials; available at floral and craft shops.

Staple gun   For attaching fake fur to plywood; available at hardware stores.

Styrofoam (cones, balls, flat pieces)   Many uses; available at floral, craft and dime stores. (If you spray Styrofoam, make certain the paint can specifies "for use on Styrofoam," or your form will shrivel and twist.)

Vise   Handy for holding wood while sawing; available at hardware stores.

Wooden plaques, boxes and shadowboxes; available at craft and other shops.

The purpose of this book is to create natural designs at a minimum of cost, so there is no need for elaborate equipment. Use whatever you have and improvise wherever you can. Visit garage sales and thrift shops, and watch for local junk drives to obtain useful materials to use in your designs.

Now, begin creating your own designs, using this book as your guide.

Chapter 2
Decorative
Wood

COLLECTING

Driftwood is the term often applied to nature's castoff wood. However, in many cases, this is a misnomer. Much of what we incorrectly refer to as driftwood is actually more appropriately called *dry-ki* and *weathered wood.*

As the name implies, driftwood is wood that drifts or floats ashore. These pieces are found along seacoasts and salt water inlets. Here, the beached wood is blasted by wind-swept sand, which often creates grotesque shapes out of the salt-washed wood. Exposure to the sun and blowing sand also enhances the surfaces of the wood with soft patinas.

Dry-ki is the wood commonly found in huge piles along many lakeshores and riverbanks. Many pieces have smooth satin-like surfaces. This wood, like beached wood, also comes in unique and unusual shapes. However, most of the pieces weigh less than the moisture-laden wood found on the seashore.

Weathered wood is found in various places and has numerous origins such as the weathered beams, shingles and boards from old barns, houses and ships. Weathered limbs, trunks, bark and roots are additional sources.

So you see, you don't have to go to the seashore to find interesting pieces of decorative wood. Instead, your sources are endless: a woodland, a mountaintop, a field, an old farm, a roadside, a riverbank or even a desert. I've found that when I least expect to discover a unique piece of decorative wood—there it is!

Decorative wood is sold in garden stores, floral shops, wayside stands (in certain areas of the country) and even by mail order. However, half the fun of being creative is to find your own pieces!

Each piece of decorative wood is unique so that when you find a piece, study it carefully. Hold it up and view it from different angles to see if it has possibilities for a future design. (Let your imagination run wild for a few minutes while you are deciding.) Then if the wood pleases you, make certain that it is a quality piece which won't split as it dries. You can check this by pressing your fingers down in several places to ensure its overall firmness.

TREATING AND CONDITIONING

Always carefully check and clean all your decorative wood before bringing it into your home. Some pieces will merely need a good brushing with a stiff brush to remove any dust or loose dirt. Other pieces may require submerging in a pail of water and a vigorous scrubbing with a stiff scrub brush. Still others may need extensive cleaning such as the removal of decayed sections and a precautionary spraying with a good insect killer, if insects or their eggs are suspect.

When the wood is cleaned, allow it to dry thoroughly for at least a week; the drying time depending on the size of the piece and the amount of humidity.

Occasionally, a piece of decorative wood needs trimming or sawing. When this is necessary, the cut end of the wood requires special treatment. First, sand the cut to reshape it to a natural conformation with the rest of the piece. That is, soft rounded lines of a flowing piece of wood are never suddenly interrupted by a harsh, flat cut.

After sanding is completed, stain or rub the cut surface with paint the color of the piece of wood. This calls for a bit of experimentation, since each piece of decorative wood is unique in color as well as outline. I find that a faint-colored driftwood stain applied to a cut surface gives me a basic coat from which to further experiment, until I reach a satisfactory match.

Some people use a thin coat of shellac on their decorative wood. Others prefer wax, stain or varnish. I personally enjoy the natural tones of the wood and only in certain instances will I brighten an otherwise dull-looking piece with a bit of stain. When you first begin working with decorative wood, experiment with the different finishes to find your preference.

STORAGE

Where and how you store your decorative wood until you actually use it depends largely on the available space. I store my wood in a dry corner of the garage in clean cardboard boxes, which I get from the grocery store and cut down to size. I place just one layer of wood in each box, adding bits of newspaper or cardboard between the pieces of wood to prevent scratching.

And now for the most exciting part of decorative wood—its actual use.

COLLAGES, MOBILES AND WALL PLAQUES

COLLAGES

A collage can be any shape or size. How large or how small you make yours is determined only by the number and sizes of the pieces of decorative wood you wish to use in your design. The collage illustrated (Fig. 2.1) measures 11 by 14 inches.

Fig. 2.1

Select a firm background for your collage, otherwise it will buckle and sag from the weight of the glued-on wood. A flat piece of thick decorative wood, a piece of Masonite®, plywood or extra heavy corrugated cardboard are desirable backgrounds.

If you prefer, paint or stain the background for your collage. Next, attach a wall hanger to the back. (Adhesive wall hangers or screw eyes with thin picture wire are the most common methods used.) Perhaps you feel that some type of a frame is necessary, too. If so, add a simple frame before attaching the wall hanger.

After your basic plaque is completed, start experimenting with your design. Arrange your pieces of varying sizes, shapes and colors until you find a design which pleases you. Then work one piece at a time; remove a piece of wood, add Elmer's Glue-All or Duco Cement, press the piece into place and hold it for several seconds. Then proceed to the next piece. Allow 24 hours for your collage to dry thoroughly before hanging.

MOBILES

To make a decorative wood mobile, start by selecting a flat piece of wood with an unusual pattern. The wind and sand at the seashore rounded the soft tan piece I chose (Fig. 2.2). Even after drying, the knots remained secure.

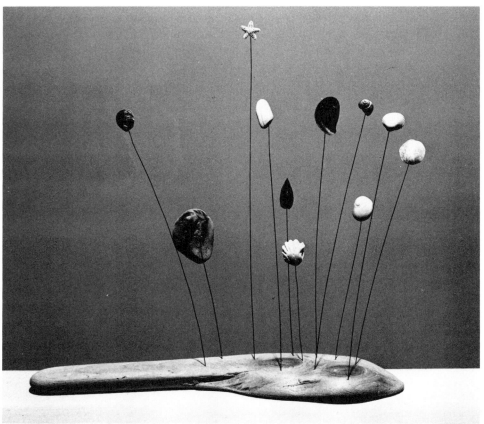

Fig. 2.2

Next, cut a number of inexpensive flexible wires to varying lengths. Flexible wire comes in various thicknesses. When using heavier materials, use heavier wires. Use Duco Cement to attach shells, small pieces of decorative wood or other seashore finds to the ends of the wires.

Determine the future positions of the wires on your wooden base and mark them lightly with a pencil. Then, using a straight pin, hammer pin-sized holes into the wood. (A small drill can also be used.)

To complete your mobile, dip the end of each wire into a drop of Duco Cement before inserting it into a hole.

WALL PLAQUES

A wall plaque can be either a simple or an elaborate project. Use any size or shape of unusual decorative wood.

The simplest method is to drill a hole into the back of the piece of decorative wood and to slip the hole over a nail hammered into the wall.

Perhaps you would like your decorative wood mounted on a simple wooden plaque to show it off. In this case, attach the wood to the plaque with screws which are put in from the back of the plaque. Then hang the plaque on the wall as you would a picture.

Larger, heavier pieces of decorative wood require sturdier mountings. For example, the piece of decorative wood shown here (see color insert) is mounted on two pieces of 1/4-inch tempered Masonite, separated by a 3/4 inch space. This allows a heavy piece of decorative wood to be hung without seeing its mounting supports.

The 67-inch "sea serpent" is attached to the outside sheet of Masonite (70-inches wide by 20-inches high); but because of its curving mid-section, it is attached in only two places (where it touches the Masonite). Long, flat head screws which pass through the spacer wood and the Masonite secure the decorative wood "serpent."

The back sheet of Masonite measures 3 inches more in each direction so that a 1 1/2-inch border of this piece is visible. A 3/4-inch-thick by 2-inch-wide spacer edging is attached to this Masonite back with screws, 3 inches from the edge.

The two Masonite pieces are joined together by four 1-inch-long, flat head screws that go through the back Masonite and into the spacer wood, which is used to hold the decorative wood to the outside sheet of Masonite.

The plaque is hung on the wall with two, 2 1/2-inch round head screws which are screwed into the wall studs but left projecting out 3/4 of an inch. Two 3/8-inch holes are drilled into the back sheet of Masonite to allow the screw *heads* to pass through. Then cut a notch at the top part of each hole just wide enough for the *body* of the screw. This secures the plaque when it is set against the wall and slipped down into place.

When all the mountings are fitted and the design completed, then the Masonite sheets are separated and the decorative wood unscrewed. The outside sheet is given several coats of flat black paint and the border of the back piece of Masonite is painted or sprayed a soft gold.

When dry, assemble again, wearing gloves so as not to fingerprint the paint when the plaque is being hung.

This is only one idea for hanging a long, extremely heavy piece of decorative wood. If you plan to copy the idea, naturally you must alter the dimensions to fit your own specific requirements.

CANDLEHOLDERS AND LAMPS

CANDLEHOLDERS

Stability is an important factor in selecting a piece of decorative wood to make a candleholder. The flat bottom of the 4 1/2-inch piece of wood (Fig. 2.3) was carefully sanded to ensure perfect levelness. In some instances, sanding is not enough, however, and a piece of decorative wood must be sawed in order to attain the levelness desired.

After the levelness of your wood is established, drill a small hole (smaller than the screw on the candleholder) down into the desired position for the holder. Then screw in an inexpensive candleholder and insert a candle.

A longer piece of decorative wood with low horizontally flowing lines makes an interesting candleholder for a centerpiece, mantle or table. With a longer piece of wood, three or more candles look attractive.

LAMPS

Decorative wood for a lamp must be selected with care. Consider its size. Is it large enough to give the needed height for adequate lighting and heavy enough to be stable? The lamp's stability depends largely on the size and contour of its base, which preferably should be a large flat surface. (If, in its natural state, it does not have such a surface, the piece must show shaping possibilities.)

The height of the piece of decorative wood is important in hiding your wiring pipe. Therefore, select wood high enough to serve this purpose (Fig. 2.4).

Next, take a lamp socket (with a shade bracket attached) and screw it onto a 3/8-inch threaded pipe. The next step is to select the exact location (or hiding place) for mounting the pipe. This detail requires considerable thought for several reasons: (1) the pipe must be mounted in a vertical position or the attached shade will always be cocked; (2) on certain pieces of wood, drilling a hole or chipping away bits of wood is necessary in order to make a proper "nesting" place to mount the pipe; (3) the pipe must make direct contact with the wood in several places so that when it is cemented in place it will remain secure.

Now establish the proper length for the pipe. In order to do this effectively, it is best to have the correct size shade to work with. (This is a matter of personal taste, but keep in mind the scale of the shade to the finished lamp. Also, remember that decorative wood usually calls for a rustic-type shade.)

Prepare the location for the pipe and cut the pipe to its correct length. Unscrew the socket from the pipe and now cement the pipe in place with Epoxy Filler Cement. Set aside for 24 hours to dry.

After the cement dries, insert the lamp cord through the pipe, wire the cord to the socket and wire a plug to the other end. Screw the socket to the pipe and set your shade in place.

Fig. 2.3

Fig. 2.4

To make a finial, drill a hole in a small piece of matching decorative wood large enough to accept the metal finial on the lamp bracket. Cement this finial to your wood. When dry, screw onto the lamp bracket.

EASY CREATIONS

Each of our decorative wood creations is unique—truly one-of-a-kind. This is not hard to understand if we stop to realize that the decorative wood or basis for our design is also one-of-a-kind. For this very reason, you can't copy a decorative wood design. You can only incorporate an idea into your own creation.

Now share with me some of my creations.

Use a small piece of unique decorative wood as a single accessory to adorn a shelf or table. Perhaps placing it on a teakwood stand or on a piece of black lacquered Masonite might show it off to best advantage.

Try a large piece of decorative wood as a "conversation piece" on the porch or patio or in the garden.

A massive piece of decorative wood might bring a rocky coast to mind. The beautiful 8-inch specimen illustrated (Fig. 2.5) here reminded me of one of the rocky cliffs on the Oregon coast where I collected it.

After studying the wood from several angles, I decided on its most attractive surface, that is, the side to be viewed. Next, I held a small metal gull in several places on the "cliff" to see where it looked the best. (These inexpensive little gulls, which come in various sizes, are sold in shops at the seashore and elsewhere.)

Fig. 2.5

Fig. 2.6

Once the positioning of the gull was determined, I marked where the two long heavy pins attached to the gull's underside would enter the wood. Then I drilled two small holes into this extremely hard wood. A dab of Duco Cement was touched onto each pin before the gull was set into place.

Decorative wood may resemble a miniature wharf or a pile. And what is more typical than a gull landing, sitting or taking off from a wooden pile? You can almost smell the salt air (Fig. 2.6)!

A naturally hollowed-out piece of decorative wood might suggest an old decayed tree. The lovely 6-inch piece shown in Figure 2.7 looked like a miniature fallen tree with a section of its root system pointing skyward.

First, I coated the inside surface of the hollowed-out "trunk" with Duco Cement. Then I pressed preserved moss into place and glued a tiny mushroom to the moss. A forest scene in miniature!

A thin, narrow strip of flat decorative wood such as the 11-inch piece in Figure 2.8 makes an attractive wall hanging.

I attached two inexpensive stems of plastic ivy with Elmer's Glue-All and placed an adhesive wall hanger on the back of the wood. (A dried arrangement or a small shell collage would also be attractive on a narrow strip of decorative wood.)

The 5-inch piece of decorative wood shown in Figure 2.9 supports a small bone china red squirrel and three tiny natural acorns in their cups. I glued these in place with a dab of Duco Cement.

Cedar woodlands are excellent places to search for fascinating pieces of decorative wood. Weathered cedar has a soft, gray patina and its wood is of a hard texture when dried.

The fallen cedar branch illustrated in Figure 2.10 suggested a miniature dead tree, standing only 18 inches high. The lower half of one side of the "tree" was hollowed-out when I found it. This became the hidden side of the tree. The base of its "trunk" was sawed level.

The very nature of a dead tree with sweeping arms stimulates anyone's imagination. In my case, I envisioned an owl. And so, I drilled a small hole (just large enough to admit the owl's head) from the outside into the upper section of the hollowed-out area. Then from the back, I slid a miniature wooden owl up into the "trunk" with a pair of long tweezers. Next, a ball of modeling clay was pressed firmly against the owl to hold the owl securely in place with only its head peeking out of the hole in the front of the tree.

Fig. 2.7

Fig. 2.8

Fig. 2.9

To give the tree added support, I cemented its base to a small piece of thin weathered wood. When this dried, I cemented preserved moss onto the wooden base to simulate the forest floor.

A piece of decorative wood with a natural knothole makes an attractive wall hanging. Glue it onto a larger piece of decorative wood and add an owl or other bird to the hole.

Natural-looking plastic fern leaves glued into an opening in the 4-inch piece of decorative wood shown in Figure 2.11 helped me to create another woodland scene.

Mushrooms are a natural accessory on decorative wood. In the woods, we so often see them growing on fallen trees and on pieces of wood (Fig. 2.12).

I use both inexpensive plastic mushrooms and real ones, which I have preserved in silica gel, to add a bit of charm to special pieces of decorative wood.

Fig. 2.10

Fig. 2.11

Fig. 2.12

The foot-long piece of decorative wood shown in Figure 2.13 was collected on a mountaintop. To adorn the wood, I used two inexpensive plastic philodendron spikes, which I tucked into the narrow opening in the front of the wood.

If you like to arrange flowers, add pieces of decorative wood to your live arrangements. At times, you can also use wood to hide a floral container.

After the leaves fall and the birds head south, watch for abandoned nests to adorn your decorative wood pieces.

Carefully remove an empty bird's nest from a tree or bush and immediately place it in a plastic bag until you get home. (Nests are havens for all kinds of tiny insects.) Before you take the nest into your home, unpack it and spray the inside and the outside several times with a good insect killer. Allow the nest to dry.

Spray the nest with several coats of clear acrylic to give the nest substance. Then with Duco, cement the nest onto an attractive piece of decorative wood. In Figure 2.14, an inexpensive artificial cardinal sits on the edge of the nest, guarding four tiny eggs formed of modeling clay.

Small pieces of decorative wood often have shapes suitable for pendant and pin creations.

To make a pendant, first decide exactly how you want the piece of decorative wood to hang. Next, drill a small hole in the wood, large enough for a thin leather or cord string. Either knot the ends of the leather or cord or stitch them together.

Fig. 2.13

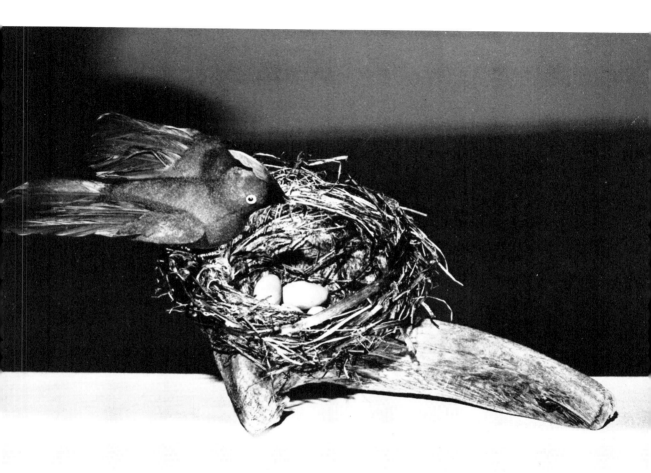

Fig. 2.14

Decorative wood pins are also easy to make. Simply glue an interesting piece to an inexpensive jewelry pin and you are all set. If you have any tiny chips of polished gems, these can be added in any natural indentations in the wood (Fig. 2.15).

Now, start creating your own designs, using nature as your guide. The world of decorative wood doesn't end here. It merely begins! The ideas for its uses are endless, as are the varied materials with which it can be used. (See the index for decorative wood ideas in other chapters.)

Fig. 2.15

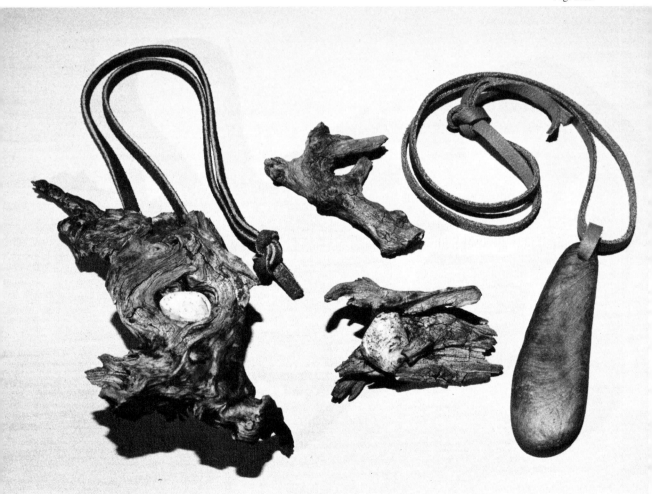

Chapter *3*
Cones, Pods, Nuts, Seeds, Pits and Berries

PREPARING

Nature offers us an endless choice of fascinating textures, patterns and shapes in the seed-carriers of plants. Parks, lots, gardens, fields and woods abound with the cones, pods, nuts, seeds, pits and berries which are the main ingredients for many of our nature designs.

In the majority of cases, our finds are nature's castoffs—empty cones or spent pods. However, sometimes our discoveries contain the seeds of life for perpetuation or for animals to feed on. In these instances, we share with nature and collect in moderation.

CONES

In most cases, for conservation reasons, collect only spent cones (those which have already dispelled their seeds.) These are usually found on the ground under trees sometime in the fall or winter. Some cone-bearing trees retain their spent cones and, in many cases, you must wait for high winds to send them earthward.

Wash all collected cones in water. Use a stiff brush to remove any hardened dirt which is in or between the scales of the cones. (Allow any cones with intact seeds to open and free their seeds before cleaning them.)

Any cones which have pitch on them will feel tacky. Remove the pitch by arranging the cones in a shallow pan lined with aluminum foil (the foil catches the excess pitch) and place the pan in a 100 to 200 degree oven for a short time until the pitch melts. As the pitch melts, some will spread over the cones, giving them a light gloss. Check the cones frequently to make certain they are not turning dark brown from too much heat. Once the pitch has melted, remove the cones from the oven. When the cones cool, they will no longer feel sticky. Then give them a thorough rinsing.

Wet cones contract, so allow spaces between the cones when you arrange them for drying. Place the cones on a piece of plastic or aluminum screening which is propped up so that air moves around them. Set in a warm place to cure. Small cones take several days to dry, while the larger kinds may take up to two weeks. Cones are dry when fully expanded and when their scales feel stiff. (Expanding cones make strange cracking noises like melting ice!)

Store cleaned, dried cones in covered, labeled boxes.

Affix cones to wood and other smooth, flat surfaces with Duco Cement. Wire your cones for use on wreaths, hardware cloth and other open designs. The size of the wire depends on the size of the cones. Usually a size 20 to 22 wire is good for large cones, while size 24 or 26 is better for smaller cones.

To wire a cone for attachment in a design, first wrap a wire around the lower scales and bend both ends of the wire toward the base of the cone. Twist the wires together, allowing a longer end of wire for attaching to your design. To wire a compact cone use a drill to make a hole through the base of the cone and insert the wire through the hole. Twist the wire close to the cone and leave the long end for attaching. If you prefer, as I often do, leave equal lengths of wire on each cone for attaching purposes.

Cut cones into sections or in half with a coping saw or a sharp pair of pruning shears.

Spray cones with clear acrylic to give them a gloss. Some cones suitable for uses in natural creations include:

Cedar or arborvitae	Hemlock	Redwood
Cypress	Larch or tamarack	Sequoia
Fir	Pine	Spruce

PODS

Collect pods mainly in the fall and winter. However, when you see interesting pods at other times of the year, take a few and experiment with the color differences when they are dried at various stages. For the most part, though, collect pods after the seeds are spent.

Dry long-stemmed pods by hanging them upside-down in an arid, well-ventilated place. Dry individual and short-stemmed pods on a piece of plastic or aluminum screening which is propped up to allow free circulation of air above and below the drying pods. Small pods dry in a few days; large pods require up to two weeks. Pods are dry when they feel firm and when the flesh of the pods has become woody.

Store your dried pods in labeled boxes with a few mothballs added to protect them from insects.

When attaching your pods to flat surfaces, such as plaques, use Duco Cement to hold them in place. Wire all pods when they are used on hardware cloth, wreaths and other such designs.

The weight and type of wire to use for wiring a pod depend on the size of the individual pod. For an average size pod, use about a size 22 wire. For a smaller pod, use size 24 or 26 wire. The size of the wire is a personal choice. However, the finer the wire, the easier it is to work with. Unfortunately, a large pod needs heavy wire to firmly secure it to an open design.

Wire any pod, where you have at least a 1/2-inch stem, by wrapping one end of the wire tightly around the stem. The other end of the wire is used to attach the pod to the frame of the design. For a stemless pod, drill two small holes near the base of the pod and pass a wire through. Twist the wire and use the long end for attaching purposes.

There is an endless selection of interesting pods which we can use in natural designs. These are but a few:

Acacia	Gum, sweet	Okra
Ailanthus	Iris	Poppies
Alders	Jimsonweed	Princess tree
Baptisia	Locusts	Roses
Burdock	Lotus	Sensitive ferns
Buttonbush	Magnolias	Sycamore
Castor bean	Mallows	Trumpet vine
Catalpa	Maples	Tulip tree
Coffee tree, Kentucky	Milkweeds	Witch hazel
Eucalyptus	Mimosa	Yuccas

NUTS

Gather nuts in the late summer and early fall. Wash the nuts in soapy water, rinse thoroughly and dry.

Place a single layer of nuts in a shallow pan and heat them in a 100 to 150 degree oven for 20 to 30 minutes. This is usually sufficient time to kill any insects and their eggs or larvae which may be inside.

After the nuts cool, place them in storage cans with a few mothballs. (Cans are better than boxes because nuts are a favorite of rodents.)

Duco Cement is a good adhesive for attaching nuts to flat surfaces. For open designs which require wiring, use a hot needle or a drill to make the holes in the nuts.

To wire a nut for use, pass a size 22 or 24 wire through the hole you made and twist the wire close to the nut. The long end of the wire is later attached to your design.

Spray nuts with clear acrylic for lustre. Nuts to use in natural designs are:

Acorns	Chestnuts or horse	Peanuts
Almonds	chestnuts	(legumes)
Beechnuts	Hazelnuts	Pecans
Brazil nuts	Hickories	Walnuts

SEEDS

Wash all seeds in soapy water to remove any fleshy parts. Rinse the seeds and spread them in a single layer on a cookie sheet. Place in the oven at 100 to 150 degrees for 15 minutes to kill any insects within the seeds and also to prevent germination of the seeds.

Allow all seeds to dry thoroughly and become hard to the touch before storing them in covered cans (seeds attract mice) or before using them on plaques and mosaics. Add a mothball or two to each can.

Seeds which are easily purchased or saved from mealtime preparations are:

Apple	Grapefruit	Pumpkin
Barley	Lemon	Rice
Beans, dried	Lime	Squash
Cloves	Melon	Sunflower
Corn, decorative	Orange	Watermelon
Cucumber	Peas (dried)	
Gourd	Peppercorns	

PITS

Save all fruit pits. Clean the fleshy parts off the pits. Then wash the pits in soapy water and rinse. Place in a 100 to 150 degree oven for 30 minutes to kill any insects which might be inside. Store cleaned pits in covered cans with a few mothballs added.

The following pits are suitable for use on plaques, mosaics and in other natural designs: apricot, avocado, cherry, date, peach and plum.

Use Duco Cement or Elmer's Glue-All to attach seeds and pits to plaques, pins, boxes, mosaics and all other designs.

BERRIES

Most berries do not dry successfully. The following four exceptions are the berries most commonly used: (1) bayberry—cut leaves off stems and hang to dry for 10 days; (2) bittersweet—cut vines before the yellow castings burst open; (3) pepper-tree (Schinus)—cut in full color, remove leaves and hang upside-down to dry for about two weeks; (4) staghorn and smooth sumac—cut, remove leaves and hang to dry for about 10 days.

WALL PLAQUES, MOBILES, PICTURE FRAMES AND SEED MOSAICS

PLAQUES

Plaques consist of designs created of natural materials which are mounted on sturdy backgrounds. The backgrounds may be any shape—circular, square, rectangular, oval or long and narrow. Suitable materials for backgrounds are wood, canvas board, sturdy place mats, trays and numerous other firm surfaces. (See index for other plaque ideas.)

To create a plaque, first select a suitable background and, if necessary, cut it to size. If the background needs preparations for use such as sanding, staining or other treating, do this now.

In most instances, plaques are not framed so just add a picture wire, a metal ring hanger or simply drill a hole in the back of the plaque to slip over a nail in the wall.

Next, select materials from your storage boxes. Decide on a pleasing design and then, piece by piece, use Duco to cement your materials into place. Place each cemented piece against the background and hold it with your fingers for a few seconds to make good contact. When your design is completed, allow it to dry thoroughly in a flat position for 24 hours.

The weathered cedar plaque shown in Figure 3.1 contains milkweed pods, sweet gum tree balls, hemlock cones, pine cones and evening primrose stalks.

The weathered cedar plaque shown in Figure 3.2 contains pine cones, acorns, acorn cups, hemlock cones, halved Princess-tree pods, tulip-tree seeds and sea oats.

Fig. 3.1

Fig. 3.2

MOBILES

To create a simple mobile such as the one shown in Figure 3.3, cut medium-weight wire into various lengths. Then, starting at the top, form a length of wire into the desired shape, using your hands and a pair of pliers. Loop both ends of the top wire.

Cut a few inches of medium-weight wire and bend it into an S-shape. Loop a cord around a nail secured into the upper framework of a doorway. Let the looped end of the cord hang a little above eye level. Hang the top piece of your mobile by the S hook onto the loop in the cord while you work on it.

Next, insert additional lengths of wire through the loops of the top wire. Loop the ends of these wires. Continue adding wires until you are satisfied with the design of your mobile.

Now the fun of creating a mobile really begins! Use 2-foot lengths of nylon fishing line or thread to attach your materials, knotting one end of the line to the cone, pod, nut or berry spike. Slip the other end of the line through the loop and make a single tie, so that you can later adjust the line for balance.

Fig. 3.3

Continue adding materials to your mobile until you feel it is completed. Then adjust the lengths of the lines and also the positions of the materials until your mobile is balanced. Knot the lines at the wire loops and cut off the excess ends of the lines.

Hang your completed mobile at eye level, or a little above, in a corner of the room where there is a slight movement of air. (See index for other mobiles.)

The mobile in Figure 3.3 includes various cones, pods, sycamore and sweet gum tree balls and a sumac berry head.

PICTURE FRAMES

Picture frames can be made for attractive pictures, greeting cards, or any other framable item.

Cut a piece of Masonite to the desired size. Drill two holes and attach picture wire for hanging.

Choose your picture or subject to be framed. Using Elmer's Glue-All, attach the object to the center of the Masonite.

Select cones, pods, nuts and seeds from your storage cans. Arrange these around the picture. When you are pleased with the design, cement each piece in place.

The mushroom design shown in Figure 3.4 is surrounded by various cones, pods, acorns, seeds and lichens.

Fig. 3.4

SEED MOSAICS

First find a suitable background for your design; cut a piece of plywood or Masonite to the desired size. Frame the wood with strips of molding if you like.

Next, select a simple design and lightly sketch it onto the piece of wood with a pencil. Decide on which treated seeds to use on the different sections of your design.

Spread a thin layer of Elmer's Glue-All with a small paintbrush on one section of your design. Use tweezers to set each large seed into place on the glue. Sprinkle small seeds into place. Then press the seed or seeds down with the tips of your fingers. Do a small area at a time, making certain that the seeds are positioned as close as possible. If you desire, as you finish each section, before the glue dries, sprinkle powdered spices or very tiny seeds to fill any openings. Allow 24 hours to dry.

When the seed mosaic is dry, use a soft brush to dust off any excess spices or tiny seeds. Spray the entire mosaic with several applications of clear acrylic or give it a coat of varnish or shellac.

The seed mosaic shown in Figure 3.5 is made of various kinds of dried peas and dried beans. Purchase an inexpensive rattan frame, either a large or a small design. Cut a cardboard backing for the design and cement in place with Duco Cement. Allow 24 hours to dry.

Select various treated seeds to fill the cardboard-covered areas of the rattan frame. Glue the seeds in place with Elmer's Glue-All. Spray with clear acrylic.

JEWELRY

PINE CONE PINS

Using a coping saw, cut a small triangular-shaped flat-bottomed pine cone into a 1/2-inch-thick slice. (Use cones from pines such as pitch, longleaf, swamp, loblolly, shortleaf, scrub and red.) Sand the cut.

If you like, spray or dip the pine cone slice in paint. When dry, paint a center for your flower; or simply spray the slice with clear acrylic to give it gloss but leave the cone flower a natural color.

To finish your pin, cement an inexpensive jewelry pin to the back (Fig. 3.6).

Use mini-plaques of wood or cardboard cutouts for pin backings. Stain or paint the background. When dry, cement an inexpensive jewelry pin to the backing. With Duco, cement on tiny pods, cones, berries and seeds.

The cardboard-backed pin in Figure 3.4 contains tiny cones, pods, berries, seeds and bits of chartreuse lichens.

ACORN PENDANT

Cement a treated acorn and its cup together. Drill a small hole into the center of the bottom of the cup. Insert a small screw eye into the hole and twist it up into the acorn cup (Fig. 3.4). Spray with clear acrylic.

To finish your acorn pendant, thread a chain, piece of yarn or a strip of thin leather through the screw eye and knot or sew the ends together.

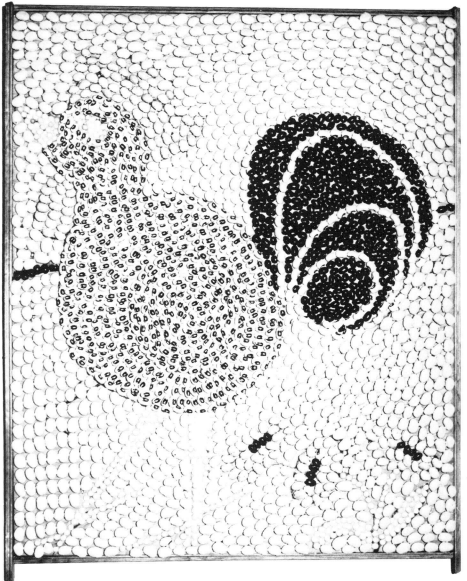

Fig. 3.5

ACORN CUP EARRINGS

Select two large, clean acorn cups of equal size. Sand the base of each cup so that it is flat.

With Duco, cement on an earring clip to the base of each acorn cup and set aside to dry. When dry, paint the inside of each cup with enamel. (A fall color is appropriate for acorn cup earrings.)

Next, choose some small dried materials with which to decorate each cup. (Make the decorations alike for the two cups.) Then cement the materials in place and set aside to dry. Finally, spray with clear acrylic.

Hemlock cones cemented to an orange background are the center for the earrings shown in Figure 3.4 and they also adorn the mini-plaque which was first sanded and then painted.

CORSAGES

To begin, select a variety of cones, pods, nuts and seeds from your collection. Choose, too, a few dried plant materials which will add a feathery touch to your completed design; perhaps statice, lichens or mosses.

Fig. 3.6

Decide on which materials to use to carry out the design for your corsage. Then, wire all your materials, leaving a length of wire to join the materials together.

After wiring the materials, cut a piece of cardboard slightly smaller than the corsage that you plan to make. (I prefer a cardboard backing except when making a small corsage or a corsage which has flat, stiff plant materials for the backing.) Now make holes in the cardboard with an ice pick wherever the wires on the materials will pass through.

After all the wires are through the holes in the cardboard, twist them together making certain that your plant materials don't shift their positions as you tighten the wires. Cut off all but an inch of the mass of twisted wires. Cover this mass with floral tape and flatten it to the backing.

Finally, add a corsage pin or wire on a small jewelry pin to the backing. If you like, embellish your corsage with a bow when designing it.

The corsages shown in Figure 3.7 contain various cones, pods, acorns, gum tree balls, lichens and artificial fall leaves.

BASKET AND DISH ARRANGEMENTS

You can use several of your treated cones, pods, nuts, seeds and berries for basket and dish arrangements. The design shown in Figure 3.8 is secured to a large coconut palm spathe with modeling clay. The arrangement consists of Princess-tree pods and buds, sensitive fertile fern fronds, gum tree balls, milkweed, alder and locust pods, pine and spruce cones, oats and beach grasses.

The small dish arrangement in Figure 3.9 is made of sumac berry spikes and statice.

PINE CONE FLOWERS AND BIRD FEEDER

With a coping saw or a pair of sharp pruning shears, slice several triangular-shaped, flat-bottomed pine cones.

The inside of the sliced cone and the bottom or underside of the cone resembles a zinnia. When you have a number of cones sliced, spray or dip them in paint. Make a number of different colored zinnias. When dry, add a bit of white or yellow paint to each zinnia center.

Use your pine cone flowers to make a plaque (see color insert). Here, a weathered cedar shake has yellow and orange zinnias cemented to it. A few sprigs of artificial foliage add softness. A thin piece of shake was sprayed green to represent the flower container.

An alternative design is a pine cone flower bouquet. Drill a small hole in the middle of the back of each sliced cone. Insert a floral wire stem and cement in place. When the cement dries, wind green floral tape around the wires. Insert the various length stems into a container.

To make a pine cone bird feeder, take a large pine cone and wind a sturdy wire around the end of the cone which was connected to a branch.

Combine bits of suet, peanut butter and a mixture of wild bird seeds. Press this mixture between the cone scales.

Fig. 3.7

Fig. 3.8

Tie the stuffed cone onto the branch of a tree, using the attached wire (preferably a branch which is easily seen from your window.)

POMANDER BALL AND BALL-SHAPED TOPIARY

Using an orange and the end of a skewer or an ice pick, make several small holes (close together) in the peel. Push a clove into each hole. Continue making holes and inserting cloves until the entire orange is covered.

The completed pomander ball will last for years. Place it in a closet or drawer to enjoy its delightful aroma or to keep away moths. Or if you desire, push a short 1/4-inch pointed dowel into the center of the orange and create your own pomander ball topiary (see Fig. 3.10).

To make a ball-shaped topiary, start with a 4-inch Styrofoam ball and a dowel approximately 1/4 inch in diameter and 12 inches long. With a knife, whittle one end of the dowel to a point. Carefully insert the pointed end of the dowel about 3 inches into the ball, making certain that the dowel points straight into the center of the ball. Remove the dowel.

From your stored materials, choose a wide selection of suitable dried materials for decorating your Styrofoam ball. Place the ball on a nest of rags with the hole side up.

Now begin decorating the Styrofoam ball. First pull a small bit of Styrofoam out with a tweezer in order to make a nest for the first piece of dried material. Squeeze Elmer's Glue-All into the nest and press the piece of dried material into place. Continue onto the next piece of material, making certain that the hole in the ball remains uncovered. Insert bits of preserved moss or lichens between the pieces of dried materials so as to completely hide the Styrofoam. Cover the base and lower half of the ball.

When the lower half of the ball is covered, set the ball aside for 24 hours to dry on its nest of rags.

The next day, drill a hole in a scrap piece of flat wood and insert the blunt end of the dowel. Carefully place your half-decorated ball over the tapered end of the dowel. Now complete decorating the upper half of the ball in the same manner as you did the lower half. Allow the ball to dry for 24 hours.

Fig. 3.9

Meanwhile, take a 3-inch clay flowerpot or other container; and with wire snips, cut several circles of hardware cloth to fit into two or three levels of the pot. Cut a small circle in the center of each circle to allow for the dowel which must stick straight up in the center of the pot.

When the decorated ball is dry, decide on the proper length for the dowel, taking into consideration that several inches will be hidden in the container and several in the ball. Slip the decorated ball off the dowel and set it on a nest of rags. Pull the dowel from the wood and saw the dowel to the desired length.

Next, cover the part of the dowel which will be the trunk, or exposed part, with Elmer's Glue-All. While the glue is still moist, sprinkle a mixture of small bird seeds (or whatever you wish to use to represent bark) onto the glue. Set the dowel aside to dry.

When the bird seed on the dowel is dry, hold the dowel by the pointed end and slip it through the center holes in the layers of hardware cloth in the pot.

Mix a small amount of plaster of Paris and pour it into the pot. Make certain that no air pockets are caught in the plaster. As the mixture sets, make absolutely certain that your dowel is perfectly firm and straight. After the plaster starts to set, allow 24 hours before finishing your topiary.

Finally, squeeze a few drops of Elmer's Glue-All into the hole in your decorated ball and set the ball into place.

When you are certain that all the moisture from the plaster of Paris is gone from the clay of the pot, then paint the pot to your liking.

After the paint on the pot dries, cover the plaster of Paris with preserved moss or pretty pebbles.

The ball-shaped topiary illustrated here (see color insert) is covered with acorns and their cups; small cones and pods; pearly everlasting flowers; and various mosses and lichens.

(See the index for other cone, pod, nut, seed and berry ideas.)

Fig. 3.10

Chapter *4*
Dried Flowers, Plants and Insects

DRYING PLANT MATERIALS BY THE HANGING METHOD

Today we dry flowers and foliage by the hanging method as did many of our colonial ancestors. It is still the easiest of all the flower drying techniques. However, not all flowers, for example, those with large fleshy flower heads, can be dried in this manner.

These are a few of the common plant materials which respond well to the hanging method:

Artemisia	Goldenrod	Pussy willow
Baby's breath	Honesty	Salvia
Cattail	Hydrangea	Statice
Celosia	Joe-pye-weed	Strawflower
Chinese lantern	Lavender, sweet	Tansy
Dock	Mullein, common	Yarrow
Globe amaranth	Pearly everlasting	

Some grasses and grains to hang are:

Barley	Marsh grass	Quack grass
Beach grass	Millet	Rye
Beard grass	Oats	Sorghum
Crab grass	Orchard grass	Timothy
Foxtail grass	Pampas grass	Wheat

For calico, Indian, rainbow and strawberry corn spread the husks open to dry.

(If you cannot raise or are not able to pick the common plants listed for hanging, try your local florist or garden shop for this material.)

To process flowers or foliage by the hanging method, pick the materials between the time when they are one-half open to just before they fully mature. At this stage, flowers are usually in prime color.

Cut the flowers or foliage in the afternoon on a sunny day when they are free from dew or other moisture. If possible, allow 12 to 16-inch stems. Immediately after cutting, defoliate the stems of flowers.

If the flowers or foliage are wilted when you get them home, simply snip off the tips of the stems and insert the stems in water until the plants revive.

Next tie the stems tightly, with rubber bands or cord, either singly as in the case of large-stemmed plants or into groups for thin-stemmed kinds. Spray with a fine mist of insect killer. Hang upside-down in a warm and dry, dark, well-ventilated area.

Before hanging some of your flowers, you may want to replace the real stems with floral wire stems. This is often preferred because the wires allow the stems to be bent into desirable positions when the materials are used in arrangements. Wire stems are a necessity on strawflowers and globe amaranths.

To substitute a wire stem for a natural one, cut off the real stem and insert a floral wire up through the base of the flower. Allow the wire to extend several inches above the flower as you bend the end of the wire to make a 1/4-inch hook. Then pull the wire from the base until the hook becomes embedded in the flower head. Wrap the wire with florist's tape.

The drying process takes from four days to two weeks depending on the kind of plant material which is being dried and on the amount of humidity. Plants are dry when their stems snap and the plant feels stiff when touched.

When dried, loosely store the different kinds of plant materials in covered, labeled boxes until ready for use in winter bouquets or other arrangements.

Experiment with hang-drying the flowers you pick from your garden or local fields and woods. You will soon discover your own favorites to use in your designs.

The arrangement shown in Figure 4.1 consists of brown dock (which was picked in the late fall) and large strawflowers.

DRIED-IN-THE-FIELD PLANT MATERIALS

In the late fall and early winter, be on the lookout for interesting dried-in-the-field plant materials to use in your creations. After you cut the stems of the plants, turn the materials upside-down and shake to dislodge any seeds which are left. (This is a good conservation practice.)

A few common dried-in-the-field materials are:

Docks	Grasses	Steeplebush
Evening primrose	Mulleins	Teasel
Goldenrods	Queen Anne's lace	

Fig. 4.1

These are just a very few of the hundreds of usable dried-in-the-field plant materials which are found along roadsides, fields and gardens. Sometimes they are so common that we overlook their potentials.

The curved leaves of grasses and the handsome spikes of steeplebush are combined in Figure 4.2.

BASKET PLATE HOLDER

Spray an inexpensive basket plate holder the desired color for your design. Pass the ends of a small piece of wire from the front, around through a bit of basket weave to the back. Form the ends of the wire into a small hook for hanging the basket on the wall.

Attach your dried material arrangement with Elmer's Glue-All. If you can find a colorful butterfly, or can buy one, glue it in place to add interest to your design.

The green sprayed basket illustrated here (see color insert) contains grasses, strawflowers, evening primrose stalks, wild rose hips and a monarch butterfly.

GLASS JARS

Decorative glass jar containers come in all sizes, heights and shapes. Select one suitable for your purposes.

Fig.

If working on a tall narrow glass jar, use long tweezers to work on the arrangement. First press a piece of modeling clay securely to the inside base of the jar. Cover this with preserved moss, sand or small pebbles.

Tall slender plants such as wheat, grasses and spiked flowers are best for the tall jars. Shorter plant materials are then graduated downward toward the base. Press all the plant stems firmly into the clay.

Small terrarium jars are ideal for showing-off small dried flowers and foliage. Again press in clay, add a covering for the clay and then push the stems of the dried materials in place with tweezers.

The dried flower terrarium in Figure 4.3 contains a blanket of preserved moss and small dried flowers.

SHADOWBOX PICTURE

Buy a small inexpensive shadowbox in a craft shop or use a shallow cardboard or wooden box in its place.

Sand the box if necessary and then paint or stain it. Use one color or, if you like, paint the inside of the shadowbox with a contrasting color.

Next, press a small lump of modeling clay at one of the inner corners of the shadowbox. Push the ends of your plant materials into the clay to make an arrangement. Cover the clay with dried foliage and stones or perhaps use the clay in a miniature vase which is securely fastened to the inside of the shadowbox with Stickum.

The shadowbox in Figure 4.4 contains dried-in-the-field bush clover and dried grasses.

PEARLY EVERLASTING TOPIARY

A 2-inch diameter Styrofoam ball is used to make the small topiary shown in Figure 4.5. First, if you like, spray the Styrofoam ball with gold Styrofoam paint; if not, leave the ball white.

Insert a 6-inch piece of 1/4-inch dowel (sharpened to a point at the end which is to enter the ball) halfway into the Styrofoam. Make certain that the dowel points straight up into the center.

Next, place the Styrofoam ball in a small nest of rags. Now attach dried pearly everlasting flowers with Elmer's Glue-All. Allow a section at a time to dry before turning the ball around to work on another part.

Once the entire ball is covered and the glue dries, temporarily insert the flat end of the dowel into a piece of modeling clay or a hole drilled into a piece of wood. Spray your topiary and its trunk with a coat or two of gold paint, if you like, or leave your flowers their natural color and stain the trunk.

Before you cut the dowel to its correct length, view your topiary with its container. Decide on a favorable length for the dowel, making certain that you allow for the portion of the dowel which will be inserted in the base of its container. Then mark the dowel and saw it straight across.

Modeling clay is usually all that is necessary for positioning a miniature topiary in its

Fig. 4.4

Fig. 4.5

container. If not, you can use plaster of Paris. After packing the modeling clay solidly into the container, insert the flat end of the dowel, pushing it down until it comes in contact with the base of the container. Add a few chips of polished gems, pebbles or preserved moss to hide the clay. Add a ribbon and a small figurine if you so desire.

DRYING LICHENS, FUNGI AND MOSSES

Look for lichens growing on rocks and the bark of trees. Fungus and mosses are found mostly in moist woods.

Wash lichens, fungi and mosses under the faucet to remove all particles of dirt before starting the drying process.

Place small lichens like the gray or gray-green ones on crinkled masses of paper towels to dry. Set in a warm, dry place. Change the towels once a day until no moisture appears on the towels. (When dry, some lichens become very crisp and easily disintegrate when handled.)

British soldiers and pixie cup lichens dry especially well on paper towels. These unusual but fairly common lichens add interest to artificial dish gardens and terrariums. (To brighten the red tops on faded British soldiers, simply rub the tops with the side of a toothpick which has been dipped into bright red paint.)

With water and a soft brush, clean the bracket fungus which grows on the sides of trees. Dry the fungus on layers of newspapers. While it is drying, spray with Lysol to inhibit mold from growing on the moist surfaces. Large brackets often take many weeks to thoroughly dry.

Several kinds of bracket fungus have smooth, glossy surfaces on the upper sides. After these types are dried, apply a spray coat or two of clear acrylic to enhance the surface and seal any imperfections on the glossy side.

Many different types of mushrooms dry successfully in silica gel. If they fade slightly when they dry out, brighten their colors with a light coat of enamel.

Dry different kinds of moss on paper towels or in silica gel. A few kinds retain their color indefinitely, but the majority of mosses lose their color in a short time. To brighten faded moss, spray a light coating of moss green paint over it.

Preserved or dried moss has endless uses: natural covering for clay or Stickum; natural ground covering for an artificial terrarium or dish garden; colorful addition to a topiary, wreath or other design.

The large foot-long bracket of mahogany fungus shown in Figure 4.6 was sawed off a fallen hemlock tree. To prepare it for use, the cut was sanded perfectly level so that the bracket would stand like an opened fan.

After thorough cleaning, Lysol treatments and complete drying, the fan-shaped bracket was used as an interesting background for a small bouquet of contrasting artificial mums and gold sprayed fertile fronds of sensitive fern.

An inexpensive miniature wooden plaque with a jewelry pin glued to the back was used to make the pin illustrated in Figure 4.7. The plaque was sanded, given two coats of stain and then a small horse's hoof fungus was cemented in place with Duco Cement. Later, a coat of clear acrylic was applied.

Fig. 4.6

Fig. 4.7

The small piece of bracket fungus (see Fig. 4.7) serves as an unusual pedestal for a tiny wooden frog.

(For other fungus, lichen and moss ideas see the index.)

PRESERVING FOLIAGE WITH GLYCERIN AND BY DEHYDRATION

Leaves and foliage preserved by the glycerin method remain flexible and last indefinitely out of water. Unfortunately, not all foliage responds favorably to the glycerin treatment. The most successful results are achieved with foliage which has body, such as the tougher leaves of trees and some shrubs.

When selecting foliage for preservation, cut branches with few or preferably no blemished leaves. After you get your foliage home, clean the branches and leaves in water. Next, place the cuts of the branches on a hard surface and mash 3 inches of these ends with a hammer.

Mix one part glycerin to two parts water. Pour this into a narrow-mouthed container such as a milk bottle or a quart pickle jar. (The narrow opening prevents excess evaporation.) Fill the container to a depth of 4 to 6 inches with the glycerin solution.

Start treatment by immersing the frayed ends of the foliage into the glycerin mixture. Place the container in a dry, ventilated room. Check the glycerin solution daily, always making certain that the level is above the mashed ends of the branches. Inspect the leaves, too, observing the gradual change of color in the leaves. When the new color spreads to the edges of the leaves or when oozing takes place along the edges, remove the foliage from the glycerin solution. For some thinner leaves, four days completes the treatment; while for others, like the leathery magnolia leaves, a month is often required.

Galax, ivy, periwinkle and lily-of-the-valley absorb moisture through their leaf surfaces. These kinds of plants, therefore, are completely immersed into a glycerin solution. Use an old covered casserole dish as a container for complete immersion treatment.

Fill a casserole dish halfway with a mixture of one part glycerin to one part water. Place the foliage below the surface, weighing it down in several places with stones. Make certain that the casserole is covered to prevent rapid evaporation from the large surface of the liquid.

Each day check the foliage in the casserole. When the submersed leaves are almost twice as dark in color as the other parts of the leaves, remove from the glycerin mixture. Place the dripping foliage on a bed of newspapers or paper towels. Wait a few days and then gently wash the foliage in soapy water. Next, rinse in clear water and pile on newspapers or paper towels to dry.

Experiment with the different kinds of foliage which are available to you. If after treatment, the leaves are an unfavorable color, simply use a light coating of spray paint to give the desired color.

Several branches of preserved leaves can be attractive when used by themselves in an interesting container. And don't forget that preserved foliage adds that special touch to all your floral arrangements.

Seal your left-over glycerin solution (for reuse) in a labeled jar.

Here is a list of foliage which responds to the glycerin treatment:

Barberry	Galax	Oak
Beech	Iris	Periwinkle
Boxwood	Ivy	Plum
Canna	Laurel	Rhododendron
Crabapple	Lemon	Sweet gum
Dogwood	Lily-of-the-valley	Viburnum
Eucalyptus	Magnolia	Yucca
Forsythia	Maple	

The color of most of these leaves changes during treatment and also varies with the time of year at which the foliage is preserved.

WOODLAND TERRARIUMS

Press a 2-inch-thick piece of green modeling clay at the inside base of a terrarium toward the center back. With your fingers, spread a thin layer of this clay at the front and sides of the terrarium. When you are finished, the highest point of clay should be toward the center back.

Cut a piece of preserved moss to cover the clay, pressing the moss down on the edges to hide the clay.

Select preserved plant materials or natural-looking artificial ones to fill your terrarium. Press the stems of the materials through the moss and into the bed of clay below. Add a tiny mushroom or two for interest (see Fig. 4.8).

CHAMPAGNE GLASS DISH GARDEN

Purchase an inexpensive champagne glass, a plastic one may be used. If the stem is hollow, fill it with sand or pebbles.

Place a small amount of green modeling clay in the center of the glass and with your fingers smooth the clay to a thin layer at the edges of the glass.

Press preserved moss into place on the bed of clay. Add tiny preserved plants or artificial ones. In the champagne glass dish garden shown in Figure 4.9, bits of crushed quartz glued into place represent a winding brook. A tiny red mushroom adds color.

Plant materials can also be preserved by dehydration. There are many desiccants or drying agents which are used for preserving plant materials. Silica gel, borax mixtures and sand are the most common ones.

Silica gel (my preference) is a chemical compound consisting mainly of fine white granules mixed with a smaller quantity of blue granules. The "telltale" blue granules turn pink when the silica gel mixture reaches its maximum moisture content. When this

Fig. 4.8

Fig. 4.9

happens, place the silica gel into a large shallow baking pan in a 250 degree oven until the blue of the telltale granules returns. Then store the mixture in an airtight container.

Select the right drying container before starting to use your silica gel. The container should have a tight-fitting lid and should be large enough to allow ample room for the silica gel and the drying plants. Cake tins, coffee or shortening cans and plastic boxes with tight-fitting lids serve well.

Pick your flowers or other plant materials for drying on an arid, sunny day. Flowers, of course, are usually picked just before they reach full bloom, when they are in best color. However, any stage from bud to prime color can be dried. To retain their colors, start drying the flowers as soon as possible after cutting them. Use a different container for each type of flower, since the drying time varies for different kinds.

Begin by pouring a 2-inch layer of silica gel into your drying container. Then cut the flower stems to 2-inch lengths and press the stems into the silica gel with the flowers facing upward. Allow ample room between the flowers and the edge of the container so that the flowers do not touch the can or one another. (Stalk-type flowers are dried in a horizontal position.)

Now take a tablespoon of silica gel and hold it about 4 inches above the level in the container, allowing the mixture to slowly trickle around the inside edge of the container. When the silica gel is about 1-inch high around the edge, tip the container first one way and then another until granules of silica gel shift around the bases of the materials to give them support. Once this is accomplished, trickle silica gel on top of the plant material, allowing it to get around any petals until they are completely covered. When the plant material is no longer visible, add another inch of silica gel.

Replace the tight-fitting lid on the container and seal it with masking tape. Label with date and name of contents. The drying times vary from two to eight days, depending on the texture, size and maturity of the individual plant.

Finished desiccant-dried plant material is crisp. If it is left in the silica gel mixture too long, it falls apart. To avoid this, uncover part of the material every day in order to feel its state of stiffness. Remove when it first feels crisp to the touch.

When dried, remove the plant materials by slowly and carefully pouring off the silica gel mixture. Then lift out the plants and carefully blow off any particles which remain. Use an artist's brush to help remove any tiny flecks of silica gel dust.

Store your desiccant-dried plant materials in sealed, airtight jars or other containers until ready to use. Add a few tablespoons of silica gel to each container as a moisture preventative.

To use your desiccant-dried flowers and foliage, with florist's tape, attach a florist's wire onto the 2-inch stem which you left on the flower. (If you prefer, this operation can be done before beginning the drying process.) A drop of Elmer's Glue-All may be needed to glue on a broken petal or stem.

Desiccant-dried flowers and foliage can be used for floral arrangements, winter bouquets and small glass-enclosed ornaments. Where humidity is an important factor, a clear acrylic sprayed onto the dried plant material often helps to reduce drooping due to excess moisture in the air. Of course, too, protect dried materials from direct sunlight and other strong light sources to retard the loss of their colors.

Borax alone dries plant materials too quickly and, therefore, needs constant attention. For a more satisfactory borax desiccant, mix two parts borax and one part white cornmeal or one part borax to one part yellow cornmeal. Mix in three tablespoons of uniodized salt to each quart of borax mixture.

The directions for using borax mixtures are much the same as for using silica gel. However, leave the drying container uncovered during the drying process. The drying time varies from 10 days to 2 weeks.

Very fine-grained sand which is first sifted and then thoroughly washed and dried also can be used as a desiccant. The directions for silica gel apply here also.

Place the sand in a covered box lined with waxed paper and allow anywhere from 10 days to 2 weeks for the covered plant materials to dry.

Plants which do well in desiccants are:

Ageratum	Daisies	Mosses
Asters	Delphinium	Mushrooms and fungus
Azaleas	Feverfew	Narcissus
Bachelor's buttons	Goldenrod	Pansies
Black-eyed Susans	Gladioli	Peonies
Candy tuft	Hollyhocks	Queen Anne's lace
Carnations	Hydrangea	Roses
Chrysanthemums	Larkspur	Snapdragons
Crocus	Liatris	Stock
Daffodils	Lupines	Tulips
Dahlias	Marigolds	Zinnias

PRESSING FLOWERS AND FOLIAGE

The most desirable flowers to press are those which lie flat and which have thin, light-weight blossoms. Those with stout pulpy flowers or those with large, thick button-like centers can't be pressed successfully.

Cut flowers for pressing just before they fully mature, since at this stage they are at peak color. Gather flowers or other plant materials after noon on a sunny day when they are free from moisture. Select only the most perfect flowers and foliage, avoiding blemishes and insect holes. In most cases, cut the flowers off their stems and then cut the stems and any significant foliage wanted. Press the stems and foliage separately and later reassemble when the flowers are used.

Flowers with clusters of florets, such as goldenrod, often need scissor trimming in the back of the flower heads to make them flat enough to press. Large flower clusters like geraniums should have their individual florets pressed and then later reassembled to form the flower.

There is no one correct way to press flowers and other plant materials. Everyone develops his or her own special pressing techniques which are geared to fit individual needs.

I never go hiking without an old pocket-sized book (held tightly together by two rubber bands) and a small pair of scissors tucked into my pack. When I see pressing material, I snip off what I need and insert it (usually face down) between the pages of my book.

When I return home, I transfer my plant materials into old telephone books, which I have always found sufficiently absorbent for my needs. I leave several empty pages between the materials so that the pages don't get bumpy, causing my materials to dry unevenly.

The telephone books are then weighted down with an old sewing machine. After 12 hours, I check my materials and place them on the dry pages in another phone book.

Since some of the moisture in the materials is first absorbed in my pocket-sized collecting book, usually only one change is needed between telephone books in order to remove additional moisture from delicate specimens. However, if I do find that my drying materials show signs of moisture when I transfer them to the second book, then in 24 hours I change them again to a third book. Of course, all during this initial drying process, the books are weighted down.

When moisture no longer shows in the materials which are being pressed, I simply weight the books and set them aside, checking every few days to make certain that the materials are drying properly. I allow about five days for small thin flowers to dry and ten days or longer for large, many-petaled flowers. (Dried flowers are crisp and remain perfectly flat when picked up.)

Some persons prefer a plant press to the book method for preparing their press materials. To make a press, cut two pieces of 1/2-inch plywood that measures 9 by 12 inches or 12 by 17 inches. Cut newspapers and fold these to the size of the press. The plant materials are then placed face down between the newspapers. (Don't use paper towels because they leave texture marks on the pressed materials.) Cut several sheets of corrugated cardboard (with a one-edged razor blade) to the size of the wooden boards. Place these every inch or so between the newspaper layers to act as ventilators.

Apply pressure to the plant press by pulling two straps or belts tightly around the outside of the plywood boards.

Most magazines do not make good plant presses because their pages are not absorbent enough. However, if you use several thicknesses of newspaper between every four or five pages of a magazine and place your materials between the newspapers, then you can use magazines. (Cut the newspapers an inch smaller than the pages in the magazine.)

Place the magazine or magazines between two plywood boards 1/2-inch thick and measuring an inch or so wider and longer than the magazines. Now weight the boards down with a heavy object, but check the materials daily.

Store small quantities of pressed flowers or foliage in labeled envelopes, hosiery or handkerchief boxes. Always store your pressed materials in a dry place and add a mothball or some moth flakes to discourage tiny insects from disturbing your materials.

Some kinds of flowers always retain their colors when pressed; other flowers gradually fade. Often, for some unknown reason, a certain kind of flower which in the past always pressed beautifully suddenly turns out a disaster. Perhaps the flower was picked past its prime or the drying process was faulty. Sometimes we never find out what went wrong. However, the more we experiment with pressing plants, the more our successes outweigh our failures. Plant materials suitable for pressing include:

Ageratum	Columbine	Hydrangea
Ajuga	Coral bells	Ivy
Alyssum	Coreopsis	Larkspur
Artemisia	Cornflower	Lavender
Asters	Cosmos	Liatris
Baby's breath	Daisies	Marigolds
Black-eyed Susan	Delphinium	Pansies
Brown-eyed Susan	Evergreen foliage	Pinks
Butter and eggs	Ferns	Queen Anne's lace
Buttercup	Forget-me-not	Roses
Calendula	Forsythia	Salvia
Calliopsis	Geraniums	Snow-on-the-mountain
Candytuft	Goldenrod	Stock
Chrysanthemums	Grains	Tansy
Cinquefoil	Grape-hyacinth	Tree leaves
Cleome	Grasses	Verbena
Clover	Heather	Zinnias

Some of the plants dried by the hanging method can also be pressed, so experiment by pressing these, too.

PRESSED PLANT PICTURES

Select a picture frame with glass and a stiff backing. Choose an antique-type frame if you are planning an old-fashioned design and a simple frame for a modern design.

Choose the background material; velveteen, linen, felt, colored paper, denim or milkweed floss are just a few suggestions.

Decide on a design and also on the pressed materials needed to carry out the design. Perhaps an oval, triangular, circular, fan, diamond or crescent-shaped arrangement is desired. Perhaps a small vase shape cut out of paper or a leaf will serve as a flower container in the design.

When the decisions are made, use a pair of tweezers to pick out the pressed materials from your storage boxes. Place the materials face up on your worktable.

Next, wash and dry the glass from the picture frame. Set it aside between two layers of paper towels. Place several dozen 3/8 to 3/4-inch brads and a pair of pliers next to the glass. (These are needed for the final assemblage.)

Cut the background to the size of the stiff backing, making certain that the threads of any fabric which is used are square with the edges of the backing. Then place a trimming of Elmer's Glue-All or Duco Cement along the edges of the stiff backing. Place the back of the background onto the glue or cement, smoothing the background out from the center toward the edges. (Some persons prefer to cut their fabric 1 1/2 inches wider on all sides. Then they place the cardboard backing in the center of the back of this material and fold the edges of the fabric over, sewing the cloth taut with large basting stitches which reach from side to side across the back of the stiff backing.)

Now to assemble the design on the fabric, first squeeze a drop or two of Duco Cement onto a scrap piece of glass or metal. With a toothpick, place a speck of cement onto the back of a piece of dried material (at its thickest part) and set it in place in your planned design. Start with the tallest flowers and those around the edges, gradually working inward as you progress. (Although some persons rely on the pressure of the glass to hold their pressed arrangements in place, I prefer to secure all my pressed materials with a tiny dab of cement.)

When all the pressed materials in the design are secured, use a soft artist's brush to clean away any tiny specks of dust from the background. Then place the clean, lint-free glass over the design.

Place the frame over the glass and slide the frame, glass and stiff backing "sandwich" to the edge of the worktable. Carefully flip the "sandwich" over. Push the small brads (which you laid out before) into the framework with a pair of pliers. Place the brads about 3/4 of an inch apart, allowing them to stick out 1/8 of an inch so as to hold the stiff backing in place.

To finish your picture, cut a piece of brown wrapping paper a little smaller than the size of the frame and glue into place on the back edge of the frame.

Pressed plant pictures fade quickly in direct sunlight, so hang them away from windows and other strong light sources. In time, some of the pressed materials will gradually fade, but this does not detract from the beauty of the pressed plant creation.

The pressed flower design illustrated here (see color insert) consists of artemisia foliage, ox-eye daisies, Johnny-jump-up, blue larkspur, pink larkspur, pansies and calliopsis. (I created this picture seven years before this photograph was snapped. Note how lovely the colors remain.)

NATURE GREETING CARDS OR STATIONERY

Purchase an inexpensive pad of colored notepaper and a package of matching envelopes. Also buy a length or a roll of clear plastic self-adhesive such as Kwik Kover or Contac.

Fold a piece of notepaper in half or to whatever size fits the matching envelope. Then cut a piece of clear plastic a little larger than the front of the notepaper. (Leave the paper backing on.)

Arrange dried plant materials right side up on the front of the notepaper. When the design pleases you, pull the backing from the clear plastic and place the plastic with its sticky side up on your worktable. Then transfer your dried materials to the sticky surface of the plastic. Make certain that the right side of each piece touches the sticky surface. Use your fingers to press each piece into place. Add glitter if you like.

Next, hold the plastic with the sticky side down over your piece of stationery. Carefully, line up the edges of the plastic with the edges of the notepaper and then gently (starting at the center) allow the plastic to make contact. Then allow both sides of the plastic to flow from the center out to the edges. When positioned, smooth the plastic out with your fingers. (By allowing the plastic to first touch in the center and then flow to both ends avoids trapping air under the plastic. If air is trapped, prick with a pin.)

Trim the excess plastic from the edges of the notepaper. The finished stationery is used for notepaper or, with the proper message printed inside, as an attractive greeting card.

Ivy, sumac and maple leaves adorn the greeting card shown in Figure 4.10.

One of the loveliest ideas for making stationery and greeting cards uses wax paper, facial tissue and glue.

To start, take a piece of folded notepaper; open it and lay it down flat in the center of a piece of brown wrapping paper cut several inches wider and longer than the opened notepaper. Next, with a pencil, carefully draw the outline of the opened notepaper onto the brown paper. Then draw a line on the brown paper which shows where the fold in the notepaper appears. This outline helps in the placement of your design.

Iron a single-ply of facial tissue to get out the creases. Set aside. Cut a piece of wax paper smaller than the brown paper, but larger than the opened notepaper. Tape this on the brown paper, over the outline of the notepaper.

Proceed by planning your design on the right half of the wax paper–covered outline. (This will be the front or cover of your stationery or card.) Then plan a small design for the lower left. (This will be the back cover of your stationery or card.) When satisfied, carefully remove your design from the wax paper and set it aside on your worktable.

In a small dish, mix one part Elmer's Glue-All with one part water. Use a small paint-brush to give a thin coating of glue to the wax paper which covers your outline. (As you work, the glue will pull away from the wax paper in places, but this doesn't matter.)

While the glue is wet, use tweezers to carefully place the pressed materials you planned to use onto the right half (cover) and then place those planned for the lower left half (back cover). Immediately cover the materials and the entire outlined area with the ironed, single-ply facial tissue.

Next, very carefully (using the flat side of the glue-covered brush), start pressing or patting the brush onto the tissue until the tissue is completely soaked. Work from the center to the outer edges, never drawing the brush over the tissue or the tissue will tear.

If you like, add a touch of silver, gold or colored glitter before setting the wet design aside to dry.

When dry, remove the brown wrapping paper. Next, slip the wax paper between two paper towels and press with an iron (wool setting). The heat causes the wax on the paper to melt, transforming the cover into a parchment-like material.

Finally, use the outline on the brown wrapping paper as a guide to either cut or tear (using a ruler along the lines) your stationery or card cover to the correct size.

To use, your notepaper or card can simply be placed into the attractive cover. Or instead, the folds of the notepaper and cover can be joined by a thin piece of ribbon passed through two tiny holes made in the creases of the cover and the notepaper.

The notepaper shown in Figure 4.10 is adorned with a fern frond and bits of colored glitter.

(See the Christmas chapter for other greeting card ideas.)

Fig. 4.10

Fig. 4.11

PLACE MATS

Measure two 12 by 18-inch sheets of clear plastic self-adhesive (Kwik Kover or Contac) or use one sheet of clear for the top sheet and a sheet of colored plastic for the bottom sheet.

Next, arrange a pressed plant material design on your worktable. Then pull off the backing from the colored sheet (or one of the clear sheets if using two clear sheets) and place it sticky side up on your worktable. Now adhere each piece of pressed material into place with your fingers (right side up on the sticky surface of the bottom colored or clear sheet).

When the design is completed, peel off the backing from the front sheet of plastic. Carefully, with the sticky side down, line up the two sheets. Then, starting at the center, allow the sheets to make contact and allow the upper sheet to flow in both directions toward the sides. Then firmly smooth the sheets together with your fingers.

Trim the place mat and, if you like, use a ruler and a permanent ink marker to outline it. Or scallop the edges as in Figure 4.11. This place mat design is made of fern fronds, Queen Anne's lace and glitter.

NATURE BOOKMARKS

Cut two pieces of clear plastic self-adhesive (Kwik Kover or Contac) to the size you want for your bookmark. Let us say, 1 1/2 inches wide by 9 inches long.

Next, plan which pressed materials to use and how to arrange them. When you have decided, remove the backing from one of the plastic strips. Lay the strip flat, with the

Fig. 4.12

sticky side up, onto a worktable. Now place your materials face up onto the sticky surface, using your fingers to press the dried materials in place.

Remove the paper backing from the second strip of plastic and carefully line it up with the first strip. Bring them together, centers touching first, and let the plastic flow out to the ends.

To complete the bookmark, trim away any overlapping plastic on the strips. Finally, with a ruler or a straight stick as a guide, outline the bookmark with ink using a waterproof, instant drying felt-tipped pen.

The bookmarks illustrated in Figure 4.12 are made with Johnny-jump-ups, larkspur, fern fronds, maple and sumac leaves and butterfly cutouts.

LEAF SPATTER PRINTS

To make a spatter print, place a sheet of white or colored paper on a piece of stiff cardboard. Next, take a pressed tree or fern leaf and pin it in place by pushing several straight pins (perfectly upright) through the leaf and the paper into the cardboard.

Next, use a can of spray paint, holding it several feet away from the leaf and the paper, to leave only a light overall spray on the paper. When dry, remove the pins and the leaf, leaving only the leaf print on the paper.

Another method for obtaining a spatter print is to dip an old toothbrush into watercolor paint or India ink. Then by rubbing a stick over the bristles of the brush (which is held about 6 inches above the paper), the paint or black or colored ink is flicked onto the pinned leaf and paper.

LEAF INK PRINTS

The most rewarding ink prints are obtained by using a hard rubber roller or brayer, printer's ink and a piece of glass from an old picture frame.

Start by placing a small amount of ink onto the sheet of glass. Then roll out the ink with the brayer until the ink is smoothed out. (This is used as the ink supply whenever the brayer becomes too dry.)

Place a leaf with the vein side up onto a folded sheet of newspaper and roll the inked roller over the entire leaf and its stem. Then lay the leaf, with the inked side down, onto a sheet of clean white or colored paper. Cover the leaf and the clean paper with a sheet of newspaper and roll again, being careful so as not to move the leaf.

Carefully remove the newspaper and the leaf to see the results. Allow the ink to dry before using the print for stationery or framing (see Fig. 4.13).

LEAF PLAQUES

For more permanent leaf prints, try securing a series of pressed leaves to a wooden panel. Then spray or stain the wood. When the leaves are removed, their interesting outlines adorn the wood (see Fig. 4.14).

Fig. 4.13

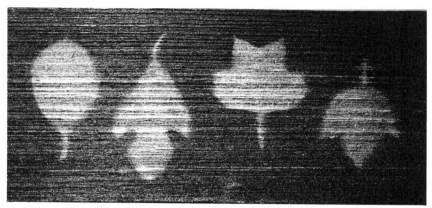

Fig. 4.14

LEAF COLLAGES ON METAL

Coat a small section of the outside of a metal waste paper pail, canister or other metal container with a glue recommended for use on metal. Place pressed leaves on the glued area, allowing the leaves to overlap each other. Repeat this procedure in order to cover the can completely. Set aside to dry for 24 hours.

Finally, spray with several coats of clear acrylic.

The decorated metal canister shown in Figure 4.15 is covered with sumac, oak, maple, blueberry and dogwood leaves in fall colors.

SPIDER WEB PICTURES

Early morning is an excellent time to locate spider webs because they are often outlined with dew. You can find orb webs in woods, fields, meadows and around old buildings. Note where the best webs are and then return to these sites later in the day when the dew has evaporated.

Before you (and a helper) start out to make your web pictures, tuck some black construction paper, a spray can of good quality white enamel, a spray can of clear acrylic, a pair of scissors and a few sheets of newspaper into your knapsack.

When you return to the spider's web that you wish to collect, inspect it carefully. Besides looking at the network of the web, notice the locations of the "guy lines" which hold the web from being blown away.

To start, if the spider is on its web, chase it away. Then, cover the surrounding area with sheets of newspaper.

Stand back from the web and spray a fine mist of white enamel first on one side of the web and then on the other. (Hold the can at least 10 inches from the web.)

Fig. 4.15

After you have coated the web with enough enamel to make the web distinct, have your helper quickly place a sheet of black construction paper behind the web, carefully positioning the paper until it comes in contact with all parts of the web at the same time. As soon as this is done, you then spray the web and paper with several light mistings of clear acrylic. The web will now stick to the black paper; cut the "guy lines" to the web before moving the paper.

Next, lay the black construction paper flat to dry. You may wish to spray the paper and web again with clear acrylic for added protection (Fig. 4.16). Place your web picture on a wood backing and glue a molding around it.

BUTTERFLY AND MOTH PICTURES

Create your butterfly and moth pictures with preserved butterflies or moths found along roadsides or in fields. (Craft stores and garden supply shops often have packages of real, preserved butterflies and moths for sale).

To use real butterflies (which you have collected) in your creations, first carefully cut the four wings off the dead butterfly at the body. (The feelers will naturally come off, too.) Handle the wings with a pair of tweezers as close to the body edges as possible, since handling the wings causes the scales to rub off.

On a piece of thin cardboard, carefully sketch the outline of the butterfly's body. With colored pencils color the cardboard the same color as the insect's body. Cut out the cardboard body.

To complete the butterfly, cut two lengths of black thread, each about 1/4 inch longer than the butterfly's natural feelers. Use Elmer's Glue-All to attach the two feelers to the back of the head section of the cardboard body. When the feelers dry, use a dab of Elmer's Glue-All to cement the four wings to the back edges of the cardboard body. Set aside to dry. [If the butterfly is to be used on a flower (see color insert) instead of in a picture, then first bend the sides of the body forward before attaching the wings.]

The large, furry-like natural feelers of moths should be glued onto a cardboard body if possible. If it is not possible to use these feelers, cut out two pieces of cardboard, color them and then glue into place on the moth's cardboard body.

If you can't find real butterflies or moths, then cut out natural-looking pictures of them. Since a butterfly's feelers are very thin and will curl when cut, replace them with glued-on threads.

Arrange your butterflies and moths on a suitable background. Then with a dab of Duco, cement their bodies to the background. Cover the picture with glass and frame.

The butterfly and moth design shown in Figure 4.17 is in a white frame with a black felt background. A white branch was first drawn onto the felt with a white pencil and then the insects were cemented into place on the branch.

Fig. 4.16

Fig. 4.17

Chapter 5
Seashore Crafts

Every walk on a beach is a treasure hunt: pretty stones, colorful shells, sand-worn beach glass, sea stars, sand dollars, bits of coral, sea urchins, tiny crabs, egg cases, claws, sponges, cork, floats, grains of sand, decorative wood and other finds. All these things and many other possibilities are the ingredients for your future seashore collages, plaques, jewelry and other creations. So, be prepared and carry a plastic shopping bag or an arm basket and a few plastic medicine vials for holding your "goodies" as you collect them.

When you arrive home from your beach walk, sort out your treasures and place them onto newspapers. For most things, simply wash in soapy water; rinse and dry and store them in labeled boxes until you use them. Some common things, however, such as "occupied" seashells, sea stars and sand dollars need special attention.

PREPARATION

SEASHELLS

Scrub all empty seashells which you find along the beach with soapy water to remove sand and salt. Be especially careful when cleaning univalves (sea snails), since sand often lodges far inside the spirals and you need to shake it free.

Give any seashell with the animal still inside immediate attention, since the longer you wait, the harder it will be to remove the body. First, place the shell in a pot of water, set it on a stove and slowly heat the water until it boils. Now turn off the flame and use a long-handled spoon to remove the shell from the boiling water. Set the shell aside until it is cool enough to handle. (Note: high gloss shells lose their sheen when boiled.)

During boiling, the muscles of bivalves (two-shelled) relax and the shells open. When cool enough to touch, scrape off the fleshy parts from the shells and scrub them in soapy water.

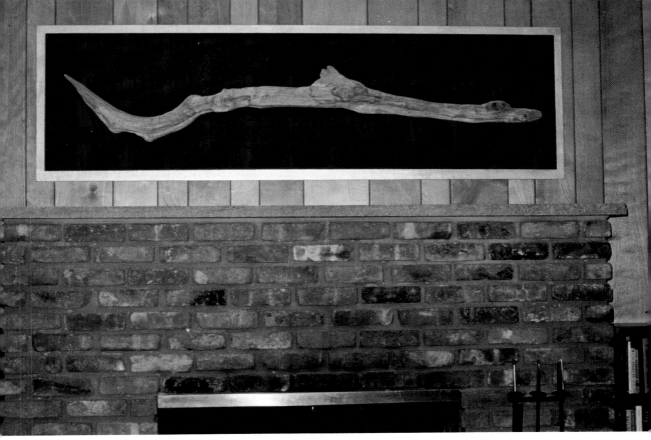

Wall plaque of decorative wood (see p. 11)

Wall plaque of pine cone flowers (see p. 36)

Ball-shaped topiary (see pp. 38-40)

Decorated basket plate holder (see p. 44)

Pressed flower picture (see p. 60)

Seashell plaque (see p. 77)

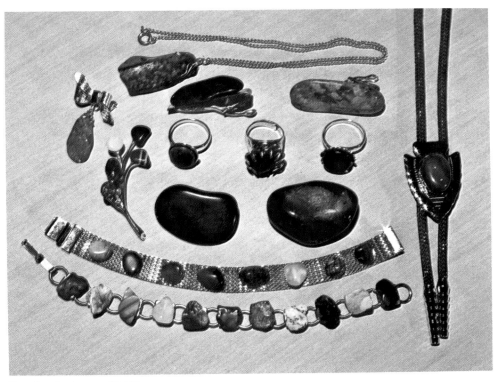

Gem Jewelry (see pp. 92-93)

Desert dish garden (see pp. 99)

Spiral cone-shaped topiary (see p. 112)

Large cone tree (see p. 112)

Fall-winter basket (see p. 133)

To remove a univalve (sea snail) from its shell, pick up the shell just as soon as it is cool enough to hold tightly in one hand. With the other hand, insert a sturdy hooked wire into the body cavity and twist the wire so that it spirals up into the shell. When no more of the wire can be inserted, pull the hooked wire out of the shell, hopefully "unscrewing" the animal's entire body as you do so. You will know if you are successful because the flesh spirals exactly like the shell, right up to the tip. It is important to free every bit of flesh with the wire or with further boiling, because even the minutest piece causes unbearable odor.

Once the flesh is completely removed, scrub the shell with soapy water. Shake water inside the spirals to get the shell cavity perfectly clean.

If your shells lack gloss when dry, spray them with a thin coating of clear acrylic. (If you intend to use your shells for gluing or jewelry, spray them after finishing your design.)

SEA STARS

It is not uncommon to find immature or adult sea stars washed ashore, particularly after storms at sea.

When you get home with the sea stars you collected, wash them thoroughly to remove all traces of dirt and sand. Then, while they are still wet and pliable, place them on several thicknesses of newspaper, arranging their arms into the desired positions. Repeat this drying operation several times within the next few hours to remove most of the moisture from the sea stars.

Finally, arrange your sea stars on aluminum cookie sheets or other flat surfaces and place in a sunny, airy window. The smaller stars harden within a few days; the larger stars take a week or longer.

Sea stars of various sizes make attractive additions to seashore scenes, plaques, mobiles and jewelry. The three sea stars shown in Figure 5.1 are cemented to a layer of orange burlap which is glued onto the glass of a picture frame.

(See index for sea star door plaque.)

SAND DOLLARS

Dead sand dollars found on the beach are often discolored. To transform them into stark white dollars, place them in a shallow dish and cover them with a mixture of one part liquid bleach to one part water. Let the sand dollars remain in the solution for several days or until they become pure white. Then rinse thoroughly.

Set the sand dollars on paper towels to dry. When dry, hold each dollar over a wastepaper pail and shake until all the dried sand within the dollar falls out from the hole on the under surface of the dollar.

Cement a sand dollar to an attractive piece of decorative wood and hang as a small wall plaque as in Figure 5.2 or set on a miniature easel. Use sand dollars to add interest to your arrangements, mobiles and collages.

Fig. 5.1

Fig. 5.2

MOBILES, SCENES, PLAQUES AND WINDOW ORNAMENTS

MOBILES

To make a simple hanging mobile, start with two sturdy wire coat hangers. With a pair of pliers, straighten the hook on one of the hangers. Now cover the two hangers with gummed tape or spray the hangers with paint.

Next, place one hanger through the other hanger in a crossed position. Then with pliers, wind the straightened hook around the hook of the other hanger until they are neatly joined. Position the crossed flat wire bases of the hangers, joining these securely at midpoint by wrapping a thin piece of wire around the two hanger bases.

Glue or wire shells and other seashore treasures to different lengths of thin wire, ribbon or cord. Experiment by hanging these at various places until you get the proper balance. Then twist or knot the ends to the hangers. (For ribbon or cord, add a drop of Duco Cement to each knot to keep it in place on the hanger.) Add a piece of coral, sponge or other large seashore find to hide the thick section where the two hooks are joined.

The coat hanger mobile illustrated in Figure 5.3 contains scallops, sand dollars, sea stars, mussels, stout and Atlantic razors, olive and jingle shells and a piece of coral.

Cork of all shapes and sizes is commonly washed ashore. A cork float found on a beach is used as the base for the table mobile shown in Figure 5.4.

To start, thoroughly wash under a faucet the piece of cork you plan to use. Let the cork dry for a day or so and then hold the piece over a waste paper pail, shaking it vigorously to get out as much trapped sand as possible.

Glue small shells and other seashore finds to flexible wires. With wire cutters, cut the wires to various lengths and insert the ends into the cork.

SEASHORE SCENES

Empty surf clam shells and quahog clam shells are very common on many beaches.

Fill a large, cleaned clam shell three-quarters full of sifted sand. Arrange a few tiny shells, a small piece of decorative wood and other bits of preserved sea life to create a miniature seascape (see Fig. 5.5).

To make a seashore scene, first select as the base a flat piece of decorative wood from your collection. In Figure 5.6, an inexpensive lighthouse grouping was cemented to the decorative wood. Then, a large piece of sand-worn beach glass was painted dark blue on its underside. This piece of glass is used to simulate the ocean. A small artificial gull cemented into place adds a special touch.

PLAQUES

First select a background for your seashore plaque: plywood, Masonite, a piece of flat decorative wood or an unfinished wooden plaque purchased in a craft store.

To start, sand the plaque and then finish it with stain or paint. Attach an adhesive hanger or screw eyes and a wire to the back of the plaque for hanging purposes.

Choose your collected seashore treasures to be used and then arrange them on your

Fig. 5.3

Fig. 5.5

Fig. 5.6

plaque. When pleased with your design, use Duco to cement the pieces in place.

This purchased plaque (see color insert) was stained with two coats of driftwood stain. Then sea stars, coral, sea oats, decorative wood, operculum from a moon snail, boat, jingle, periwinkle, coquina, top, mussel, scallop, ark, surf clam, whelk and cockle shells were cemented on. Bits of chartreuse lichen were added to simulate seaweed.

If you have handy some clean, washed and dried beach sand, coat your plaque first with glue and, before the glue dries, sprinkle on a layer of sand. Allow 24 hours to dry and then shake off the excess sand. Now cement your seashore materials to the sandy surface and spray with clear acrylic.

The sand-covered plaque illustrated in Figure 5.7 contains sea stars, coral, clam, ark, ear, mussel, moon, olive, periwinkle, boat and jingle shells.

Fig. 5.7

The wavy surface of striated plywood used in Figure 5.8 makes an interesting texture for a seashore plaque. A young boy's seashore collection is cemented to a cut out, oval-shaped piece of special plywood. The plaque contains sea stars; baby sea horses; a string of whelk egg cases; a skate's egg case; decorative wood; horseshoe crab; a fish jaw with teeth; and ear, venus clam, boat, coquina, jingle and scallop shells.

Make several plaques of different sizes and shapes. Arrange these into an interesting wall grouping.

Use a small shallow can, such as a sardine or pimento can, to make a miniature shadowbox. Paint the can and then cement seashore finds inside. Hang with an adhesive hanger.

BEACH GLASS WINDOW ORNAMENTS

Collect and save sand-worn beach glass, especially the colorful pieces, whenever you find it.

Fig. 5.8

Fig. 5.9

For the backing on a window ornament, use the clear plastic cover from the large size Cool Whip or any plastic cover of similar size. With an ice pick, punch a hole at the edge of the cover so that you can later insert a wire or ribbon to hang your ornament.

Select enough sand-worn beach glass from your storage boxes to fill the surface of the plastic cover. Next, set the container cover with the underside up onto your worktable. Coat the underside of the cover with an even layer of Elmer's Glue-All. Now press pieces of different colored sand-worn beach glass into the glue. When all the pieces of glass are in place, sprinkle clean, sifted beach sand on the cover to fill the openings between the pieces of glass. Allow 24 hours to dry before shaking off the excess sand.

Thread the hole in your window ornament with wire or ribbon and then hang where the sunlight will bring out its beauty (Fig. 5.9).

Sand-worn beach glass also makes attractive jewelry. Cement a bell cap to each piece, add a jump ring and attach to a bracelet or necklace.

SHELL CREATIONS

PENDANTS

Univalves such as olive, whelk and conch (see Fig. 5.10) are really sea snails. These and many other different kinds of univalves wash ashore, so use the ones common to the beaches you explore.

Start with a clean, sprayed univalve (use clear acrylic). Take a small piece of medium wire and, using a pair of pliers, bend one end into a small loop. The loop should be large enough to allow a thin strip of leather or a piece of cord to pass through. (This loop will be the only wire visible on the finished pendant.)

Carefully work the other end of the wire into the shell until it hooks onto the inside swirls of the shell. When the wire has a place to hold, squeeze several drops of Duco into the shell cavity to cement the wire securely inside the shell.

Prop the drying shell on a nest of modeling clay. Allow 24 hours for the cement to dry.

Cut yarn, leather or cord to the desired length for your pendant. Pass one end of the material through the wire loop on the shell and then knot or sew the two ends together to finish the pendant for wearing.

JEWELRY

With Duco Cement, attach two small attractive shells to a pair of earring screws or clips, or cement a small bell cap to each shell and use on a hanging earring finding.

Buy a miniature wooden plaque in a craft shop. Sand and paint or stain the plaque. Cement an inexpensive jewelry pin to the back of the plaque. Then cement tiny shells on the front of the plaque. When dry, spray the entire plaque with clear acrylic.

The pin shown in Figure 5.11 was finished with driftwood stain and then tiny colorful coquina shells were cemented on.

To make a shell necklace, first use a sharp ice pick to make a hole in the thin shells. Press down on the shell with the ice pick and then use your hand or a hammer to tap the pick. (Make holes in thick shells with a power drill.)

Tap two holes at one end of a handful of jingle shells. Thread the shells onto dental floss to make a simple necklace.

Preserved sea stars and sand dollars can be used for jewelry, too. Three tiny sea stars are cemented to a flat beach stone (Fig. 5.11) to which a jewelry pin is cemented.

FLOWERS

To make a shell flower, choose a flower design and the shells you will need to carry out the design. To start, spread a thin coating of Vaseline on a section of an old plate or a piece of glass. (The Vaseline eases the removal of the finished flower from the surface.) Now squeeze several drops of Duco Cement onto the coating of Vaseline on the plate or glass.

Next, form your flower on the cement by using tweezers to first place the outside shells or petals and then the inside ones. Add a pebble or a tiny shell as a center, if the

Fig. 5.10

Fig. 5.11

flower design calls for one. Press the finished flower carefully with your fingers to ensure good contact between the shells and the cement.

After the cement dries, pass a single-edged razor blade under the cement and cut your flower away from the surface.

Individual shell flowers glued to inexpensive jewelry pin or earring findings make lovely accessories.

Groups of shell flowers can be made into floral arrangements and then cemented to a wall plaque, shadowbox or even the cover of a wooden basket pocketbook.

To make a shell dogwood flower such as the one in Figure 5.12, select four small round shells. Overlap the four rounded shells on drops of cement, making certain that the shells are hollow sides up and that their hinges are on the outside. Cement a tiny round pebble or shell to the center. Press the center of the flower with your finger to make certain that all parts and cement are in contact. Set aside to dry.

When dry, finish your dogwood flower by touching each hinge with a dab of brown paint. Also paint the entire pebble or tiny shell in the center. After the paint dries, cut your flower from your working surface.

To make the shell pansy shown in Figure 5.12, select five small round shells. Overlap two of the shells on drops of cement. Then overlap two more shells directly below these. Fnish by adding the bottom shell to complete the pansy. Press with your finger and then allow to dry.

When dry, use paint and a thin brush to draw on a pansy face. Then cut the pansy from the working surface.

Fig. 5.12

ASH TRAYS, CANDY DISHES, SOAP DISHES AND PIN HOLDERS

Large cleaned abalone shells make excellent ash trays and candy dishes. They need no protective coating.

Shells such as clams, cockles, scallops and buttercups can also be used for small ash trays, candy dishes, soap dishes and pin holders. However, when using these shells for ash trays, first coat them with spar varnish to protect their finishes.

Spray a cockle shell with gold paint. Glue a small piece of felt-covered cork or Styrofoam to the inside of the shell and use as a pin holder.

Decorate shell soap dishes by gluing on shell flowers, bits of coral and other seashore finds.

SHELL FLOWER HOLDERS

Select a large, cleaned whelk or conch shell. Insert the stems of plastic philodendron or ivy leaves into the opening of the shell. Arrange the leaves to drape on the outside of the shell. A large spiral shell also makes an attractive base for a floral arrangement. Use large flat clam shells for dish gardens.

SHELL CANDLEHOLDERS

Take two clean cockle shells of the same size. Set them on your worktable with the hollowed side of each facing upward. With an ice pick and a hammer tap a small hole near the hinged end of each shell. Then turn the shells over and, using a 7/8-inch drill, make a hole in each shell at the place where the ice pick broke through. (The ice pick hole prevents the drill from slipping on the shell's surface.)

Sand each hole to smooth any sharp edges and then spray the candleholders with clear acrylic or paint. Slip in medium size candles (Fig. 5.13).

SHELL ANIMALS

Empty moon shells can be found on many beaches. To make the hedgehogs shown in Figure 5.14, take several cleaned moon shells of different sizes. Cement, above the pointed tip of the shell, two plastic or button eyes. The tip of the shell simulates a nose. Then draw a large mouth and some spines on each shell, using a black waterproof felt-tipped pen.

An unusual piece of decorative wood found at the beach led to the creation of the ostrich shown in Figure 5.15.

To make a shell ostrich, use a cleaned cockle shell for the body. (Cockle shells are common shells to find.) Set the shell with the outside resting on your worktable. Then take an ice pick and place it a short distance from the hinge of the shell. Tap the ice pick with your hand until you make a hole large enough to insert a neck for the ostrich. In my creation, the decorative wood naturally formed a perfect neck and a head with an opened bill. However, the neck can easily be made from a pipe cleaner and the head from a small shell. To complete the head, cement on two plastic or button eyes.

To make the ostrich's legs, take a foot-long pipe cleaner and form it into a large V. With masking tape or modeling clay, affix the bent part of the V to the wide underside

Fig. 5.13

of the cockle shell. Then bend the sides of the V forward to form legs. Bend the ends of the pipe cleaners again to form feet. Cement the feet to a small piece of wood. Cover the wood, if you wish, with preserved moss.

Using your shell finds, create your own whimsical animals. Use cement or Stickum to add tiny shells for feet, ears, eyes or a nose (Fig. 5.16).

Dried, empty sea urchins, both with spines and without, are found along the shore.

The spined urchin monster in Figure 5.15 was created with two plastic eyes, a pebble nose and a pipe cleaner mouth.

SHELL BOXES

From a craft shop, purchase an inexpensive box with a recessed top. Sand the box lightly. Then paint or stain it to your liking.

Cut a piece of felt (or heavy burlap) to fit the recess in the cover of the box. Spread Elmer's Glue-All onto the recessed area and press the felt into place.

After the felt is dried, arrange tiny shells or other small seashore finds on the cover. When satisfied with your design, glue the pieces in place on the felt.

The box shown in Figure 5.17 is painted gold and has black felt adorned with colorful coquina shells.

Try covering an entire box with tiny shells and then spraying the box with clear acrylic for luster.

Fig. 5.14

Fig. 5.15

Fig. 5.16

Fig. 5.17

Chapter 6
Rocks, Gems, Pebbles and Sand

COLLECTING

All 50 states have something to offer the rock hound. If you check with your local lapidary shops and mineralogy clubs, you can find the best areas in which to collect.

The equipment you need for rock collecting is simple: a rock pick with a square hammer head on one end and a sharp point on the other; safety glasses to protect your eyes from flying chips; old gloves to protect your hands; and a knapsack for carrying your loot. If you like, add a cold chisel, a small shovel and a sledgehammer to your rock collecting tools.

When traveling to unfamiliar places, your rock hounding is always more fruitful if you plan ahead. Write to the chamber of commerce in the state or states which you plan to visit and request rock hound data.

Once you arrive in a suggested rock hound area, look for road excavations, places of erosion, outcrops in cliffs and hillsides, rock dumps, quarries, deserted mines and gravel pits. All of these places, wherever earth has been disturbed, are excellent for rock hunting. (Make certain, however, that you never collect in any of our state or national parks or on private property.)

Collect unusual rocks to use for doorstops, bookends or in rock gardens. Scrub the rocks you find with soapy water and rinse them thoroughly before using them.

Create miniature nature scenes with interesting rocks. In Figure 6.1, a bone china red fox is cemented to a copper-colored rock which complements the colors of the tiny fox.

Use the pits and indentations in rocks as tiny planters. The small craters in volcanic rocks are attractive when planted with tiny succulents, or hens and chickens. The heavily pitted rock in Figure 6.2 is adorned with artificial fern.

Fig. 6.1

Fig. 6.2

PREPARING ROCKS

Collecting rough rocks is only the beginning. One day you will discover that some of the dull rocks in your collection are really semiprecious—hard rocks in disguise which, once broken into small pieces with a rock pick and properly polished in a rock tumbler, become beautiful gems suitable to be used for making jewelry.

There are many different kinds of rock tumblers, but they all work essentially the same. If you purchase one, follow your particular manufacturer's instructions.

My rock tumbler, shown in Figure 6.3, cost less than $25. This price included three packages of grits, polish, polishing pellets, an assortment of jewelry findings and 2 1/2 pounds of unpolished stones. The tumbler consists of a motor which rotates a tumbling barrel capable of holding 3 pounds of rocks.

To show you how simple rock tumbling really is, here is my procedure for polishing one batch of rocks. To start, I fill the barrel of my tumbler three-quarters full of washed rocks which I first hammered into 1/2 to 3/4-inch pieces. (Occasionally, if I am polishing for paper weights or specimen rocks, I place larger rocks in with the smaller ones.) Then I add six heaping teaspoons of coarse grit and add water to cover the top of the rocks. After screwing on the barrel cover, I set the barrel onto the tumbler. The

Fig. 6.3

tumbler runs for 24 hours a day. I open my barrel every few days to check the water level.

After 7 to 10 days, my rocks are usually ready for the medium grit treatment. If the rocks were very jagged to begin with, they may need a longer treatment in the coarse grit to wear them down. I thoroughly wash the rocks and the complete barrel. I do all this washing over a pail outdoors so that I can throw the gritty water outside rather than down the drain.

Once the rocks and barrel are cleaned, I place the rocks into the barrel again. I add 6 heaping teaspoons of medium grit and fill with water to cover the rocks. Again I run the tumbler for about seven days.

After a week, the rocks and barrel are again washed thoroughly. The rocks are then tumbled for another week in 6 heaping teaspoons of fine grit with water added to the top level of the rocks.

When the third week of tumbling is over, the rocks and barrel are very thoroughly washed to remove all tiny bits of grit. The rocks are then placed in the barrel with 6 heaping teaspoons of polishing pellets, 6 level teaspoons of polish, a 1/2-inch square of Ivory® soap and enough water to just cover the rocks. Again the rocks are tumbled for a week.

Now the four weeks are up! Again, I thoroughly wash the rocks and the barrel. Then I replace the rocks in the barrel, adding 4 tablespoons of powdered granulated detergent. I add water to within 1 inch of the top of the rocks and plug in the tumbler for about 3 hours.

Finally, I wash my polished rocks and sort them so that they are ready for use in making jewelry and other designs.

The polished gems which come from the tumbler are of irregular shapes and are called baroque gems. These lovely gems are easily made into attractive jewelry. Here's how.

GEM JEWELRY

To make jewelry out of your polished gems, first purchase some settings (called findings) from a craft store or a lapidary shop. There is a wide selection of findings available for making cuff links, pendants, rings, pins, necklaces, bracelets, key rings, bolo ties, tie clasps and earrings. These are obtainable in gold, silver or inexpensive metals. Also purchase some jump rings and flexible bell caps for attaching free hanging gems to bracelets and necklaces. A pair of jeweler's pliers and a tube or two of jewelry cement are essentials.

Next, select the particular polished stones that you wish to mount in your findings from your collection. To start, take your first finding and its gem (or gems) and decide exactly in which position to mount the gem. When you have decided, wash the finding and the gem in a detergent solution or wipe both with alcohol. Then rinse and dry. The natural oil on your fingers prevents proper bonding so handle the cleaned, dried finding and gem very carefully.

With a toothpick, apply a thin layer of jewelry cement to both the finding and the gem. Then bring the two together. Allow them to dry for 24 hours on a bed of modeling clay shaped to hold the finding in a level position.

When attaching a bell cap to a gem, shape the flexible cap to the individual gem. Then wash both thoroughly with detergent. Rinse and dry. With a toothpick, apply cement to the areas of the cap and the gem which will come into contact. Press the two pieces together and set on a bed of clay to dry.

A jump ring is used to attach a bell cap to a bracelet or necklace. Use a pair of jeweler's pliers to open and close the jump ring, always making sure that you move the ends of the ring sideways to open or close it. Never open the ring by pulling the ends in a straight direction away from each other or you will be unable to close the ring properly again. Insert the bell cap onto the jump ring and the jump ring onto a link of the bracelet or necklace; and then with the pliers, close the jump ring in the suggested manner.

Most of the gems illustrated here (see color insert) were collected on the Northwest Coast.

ROCK CREATIONS

ANIMALS AND PEOPLE

Collect rocks of various sizes and shapes. Scrub the rocks with a stiff brush in soapy water. If you plan to paint the rocks, first clean them with scouring powder. Then rinse and dry the rocks thoroughly.

To paint a rock, first draw your sketch on the rock with a pencil. When satisfied with your design, use a waterproof pen to outline it. After the ink dries, use enamel or oil to color in your design.

To complete your rock, varnish the entire rock or give it several coats of clear acrylic spray. Use the rock as a paperweight or cement the rock to a piece of decorative wood and use it as an interesting accessory.

To make the ladybird beetle in Figure 6.4, first clean a round, flat or slightly oval rock. Tip the one end of the rock with black ink (or paint). Draw a black line down the center of the rock and two large black dots on each side of the center line. Allow to dry. Then blacken the under surface. When dry, use an orange felt-tipped waterproof pen (or orange paint) to color the non-inked sections.

Cut a black pipe cleaner, or a white pipe cleaner which has been blackened, into three sections. Slightly bend the three sections you have just cut. Then arrange the three pieces on the underside of the rock (facing toward the black tip) so that they stick out on both sides of the rock to look like six black insect legs. Cement the three sections in place with Duco. Allow the legs to dry for 24 hours.

Cut two spots for eyes out of white cardboard and cement them in place on the black-tipped front of the beetle.

Set your ladybird beetle on a leaf if you like. To make the leaf, outline or sketch a large leaf onto a piece of heavy green cardboard or a piece of green felt. Cut out your leaf and, using a brown felt-tipped pen, draw in brown veins. Cement a green pipe

Fig. 6.5

Fig. 6.4

cleaner (or a pipe cleaner colored green) in place on the back of the leaf. Allow half of the pipe cleaner to show as the leaf's stem. Set your ladybird beetle on the green leaf.

A simple owl's face is painted on the round rock shown in Figure 6.5. The rock is cemented to a piece of decorative wood.

A rock pig, as illustrated in Figure 6.6, is especially fun to make. First, select a large potato-shaped rock. With Stickum or Duco, affix four small, round flat rock feet, a round rock nose, two small round rock eyes and two oval rock ears. Use a curled pipe cleaner for a tail.

Make a turtle by using a flat oval rock for the body. Then cement smaller flat rocks for feet, a long narrow rock for a tail and a long rounded rock for a head. Mark on eyes, nose and mouth with a black waterproof felt-tipped pen.

Create whimsical rock people, too. Cement the rocks together and use waterproof ink or paint to draw on the features. Add bits of cloth, pipe cleaners and yarn to dress the rocks.

The number of original animal and people ideas you can create using rocks is endless. Get started and you'll see!

CANDLEHOLDERS

As you gather collectibles, save interesting rocks which have natural holes in them. Whittle the base of a candle to the size of the hole and insert the candle into the rock. Add a bit of moss or lichen as filler around the hole. The rock for the candleholder in Figure 6.7 was found on the Oregon Coast.

Fig. 6.6

Fig. 6.7

PEBBLE CRAFT AND SAND CREATIONS

PEBBLE CRAFT

Save tiny, colorful, rounded pebbles whenever you find them. When you have enough, purchase an inexpensive wooden box with a recessed top. Sand the box and then spray it with enamel or shellac.

Coat the recess in the cover of the box with Elmer's Glue-All. With tweezers, position the tiny pebbles into the glue so that they are as close together as possible.

When the pebble-covered box dries, spray the pebbles with two coats of clear acrylic to bring out their colors and to give them luster (Fig. 6.8).

To make a pebble picture, cut a piece of Masonite to the required size or use a flat piece of decorative wood.

Attach two small screw eyes and some picture wire to the back of the wood for hanging purposes.

Draw a design on your wood with a pencil. Then coat a small section of the design with Duco Cement. With tweezers, place the pebbles closely together on the cement.

Continue cementing, a small section at a time, until your pebble picture is finished. Allow it to dry for 24 hours in a flat position. Finally, spray the picture with two coats of clear acrylic before hanging it.

Fig. 6.8

SAND PAINTINGS

Collect a small amount of sand from various beaches that you visit. Some beach sand is dark, some almost white, while other beaches have red garnet sand. The textures of the sands differ, too.

If you can't get sand from the beach, buy a small amount of sand. Divide the sand into different batches and dye each batch a different color by placing the sand in a bowl with colored ink. When the sand takes on the color you want, spread it out on newspapers to dry.

All sand to be used for sand paintings should be sifted in a strainer and washed and thoroughly dried.

To make a sand painting, first decide on the size of the design you wish to create. Cut a piece of Masonite or plywood to the correct size.

Attach screw eyes and picture wire or an adhesive hanger to the back of the wood. Frame your wood with molding if you like.

Assemble the various hues of sand which you have collected or dyed. Place each kind in an individual plastic bowl and lay out an old teaspoon for each bowl.

Draw a simple design with a pencil onto your wooden background. Then, carefully study the design, determining where each sand color will go.

Squeeze an ample amount of Elmer's Glue-All into a small plastic container. Then with a thin watercolor brush, evenly coat a small section of your design. Make certain not to allow any glue to flow outside the section that you are working on.

Using a teaspoon, sprinkle the predetermined sand onto the glued section. Shake the wood a bit to make sure that all the glued surface is covered with sand. Then add more sand to the glued section, making a thicker layer. Allow to partly dry for a few minutes. Then turn the wood over and let the excess sand fall onto a plate. (Set the plate away from the unused bowls of sand so that no foreign sand falls into the individual bowls.)

Continue by gluing one small section at a time, sprinkling teaspoons of sand, allowing the glue to partly dry and then shaking off the excess sand.

When your sand painting is completed, set it aside for 24 hours so that the glue dries thoroughly. Then spray your painting with several coats of clear acrylic.

The sand painting shown in Figure 6.9 is based on an Indian butterfly design. The design is covered with five kinds of sand.

PARFAIT GLASS DECORATION

Buy a parfait glass. Assemble various colors of clean sand which you either collected or dyed with ink.

To start decorating your parfait glass, use a tablespoon to pour in about a 1/2 inch layer of sand. Then add another layer of a different colored sand. Allow the poured layers of sand to form irregular patterns in the glass.

Continue to add layers of different colored sand (some layers thicker than others) until your top layer is about 3/4 inch from the rim of the glass. Then light a candle stub and, holding the candle on its side, allow the melting wax to drip onto the upper layer of sand. Coat the sand with about 1/2 inch of wax.

Spray the cooled wax with artificial snow to simulate whipped cream and top your parfait with an artificial cherry.

The sand parfait in Figure 6.10 consists of various colored and textured sands from four states.

DESERT DISH GARDEN

Create your own desert scene by using the interesting rocks which you find.

To make your desert dish garden, first select a shallow dish about 2 inches deep. Choose a dish of the shape, size and color that you prefer. The desert dish garden shown here (see color insert) is created in a 14-inch round, black tray.

Fill your dish with clean sand up to 1/2 inch below the edge of the dish. Arrange your interestingly shaped rocks in several locations on the sand.

Purchase small pots of cacti (or tiny succulents) and insert the pots into the sand in various places. Set your dish garden in a sunny location and water your cacti well, but not more than once or twice a week.

If you do not care for a live desert dish garden, then use green modeling clay to form imitation cacti. Model the cacti to the size and shape to best fit your scene.

To make miniature artificial saguaro cacti, like the ones in the picture, take a piece of green modeling clay and roll it between your hands until it looks like a cigar. The top end should be rounded; the other end, flat. With a pointed object, make many ridges running down from the top of the clay cactus to its flattened base. Then push the base of the finished cactus into the sand wherever you want it. Make as many cacti as you wish, but vary their heights.

After all the cacti are set in the sand, add to your desert scene some small flowers and foliage or a tiny animal, if you so desire.

(See the index for other rock, gem, pebble and sand ideas.)

Fig. 6.9

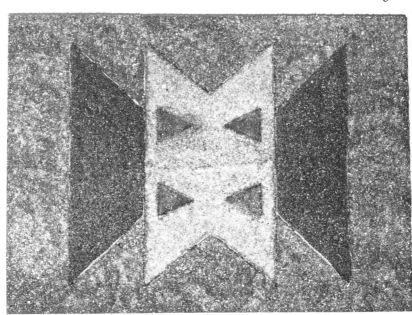

Chapter 7
Christmas Decorations

The Christmas season buzzes with a multitude of activities, so don't wait until December to plan your designs. Instead start early to work on the basic decorations, postponing only the insertion of the live greens for the very last.

Everyone has his or her favorite Christmas color combinations. When creating your designs, choose the colors which fit in with your decor.

Size is a very important factor when creating your decorations. Consider the size of the room, door or table and proportion your design accordingly. The sizes given throughout the text are merely to guide you.

HELPFUL HINTS

If you prune your evergreens shortly before Christmas, you can use them in your designs. Cut the greens either early or late in the day when the sun isn't shining directly on the foliage. Place the cut stems in a pail of water and leave in a cool, dark place for 24 hours before using. If you are unable to cut your own evergreens, you will find that most florists or Christmas tree dealers sell evergreen branches.

Be careful when using live greens in your indoor designs. Heat causes many cut evergreens to dry out and drop needles prematurely. These greens become fire hazards when used near candles, fireplaces or electric lights. Spruces and hemlocks are especially risky.

A few long-lasting evergreens which are very suitable for indoor decorations are white pine, cedar, taxus, arborvitae, juniper, retinispora, pitch pine and Scotch pine. If fresh holly or laurel is available, these also are good indoor decorating choices.

Placing the cut ends of your evergreens in water, damp soil or wet moss helps to keep the greens in your decorations fresh for a longer period of time. However, for many of your decorations, don't hesitate to substitute good-looking imitation greens along with your natural dried things.

On the average, number 22 or number 24 wire is preferable for wiring. For very small cones, pods and seeds, use a fine copper wire.

In most instances, bows are never tied in place. Instead, make the bows and then attach them to your design.

Artificial tree trunks are made of dowels, old broomsticks or plant stems. They are covered with bits of bark, bird seeds, gravel, felt or wound pipe cleaners.

When using cones, first wire them separately and then wire several together into a bunch or onto a florist's pick to be added to swags, garlands, wreaths and other designs.

If using Christmas tree balls, thread a pipe cleaner through the loop and twist. Then add to your frame or greens.

Use Stickum to hold candles securely in place.

Always wear a pair of old gloves when working with wire and evergreens to protect your hands from cuts and sap.

SWAGS, CORSAGES, GARLANDS AND WREATHS

SWAGS

A swag is used as a door, wall or mantle decoration. A single, graceful evergreen bough is often sufficient to form your swag, but usually two or three branches are needed.

White pine, juniper, spruce, arborvitae or taxus are just a few suggestions for swag material. Use each by itself or combine them; for example, a mixture of juniper and taxus makes an interesting contrast of greens.

Wire the evergreen branches together so that the swag tapers downward to a point following either a straight or a curved line. Carefully wire a few upright sprigs of evergreen foliage around the upper part of the swag to cover the cut ends of the other greens. Allow a loop of wire to pass through to the back for hanging.

Lay the swag in a flat position and, starting near the top of the swag, arrange cones or other decorative materials. Use the largest or most imposing material near the top of the swag. Gradually taper the material as you work downward. When you are satisfied with your design, wire each piece in place. Add a bow as a final touch (Fig. 7.1).

A Christmas swag can be made solely of cones. It is simple to assemble and requires only a roll of 1-inch wide ribbon. Cut the ribbon to varying lengths and tie a different size cone to each piece of ribbon. Use the shorter lengths for the larger cones and so on, so that your cone swag has the dominant material near the top. When pleased with the arrangement of cones, knot the ends of the ribbons together. Leave a loop of ribbon for hanging. A larger, wider bow of ribbon attached to the knotted ends completes the cone swag.

CORSAGES

Take a few sprigs of natural or artificial evergreen and wire them together with fine wire to form a miniature swag or a circle of greens. Cover the ends and wire with green

Fig. 7.1

Fig. 7.2

florist's tape. Wire on small cones, pods and berries. Tie on a bow and attach a simple jewelry pin to the back (Fig. 7.2).

If you make your corsage as a decoration on a gift box, add a corsage pin instead of the jewelry pin.

To make a corsage of cones, first cut a small circle of heavy cardboard and glue an inexpensive jewelry pin to the back of the circle. Next, lay five small spruce cones on the cardboard until they form a star. Stand a small cone in the center. Glue all the cones in place.

GARLANDS

A garland is a rope-like decoration for use over a mantle, mirror, archway or door. It also serves as a very handsome decoration for outlining a banister.

To make a garland, first start with a double thickness of heavy rope or clothesline which is cut to the desired length. Leave a loop at one end of the rope and secure it to a nail, doorknob or other stationary object while you work on the garland.

Next, wire together enough small bunches of 3 to 4-inch greens to cover the length of the rope. Now mark the center of the rope where the garland will be attached to the wall or framework. Starting at the free end and allowing each bunch to overlap, attach the greens with their wired ends facing upward. When you reach the center mark, start attaching the greens with their wired ends facing the center.

After you have attached all the greens, wire cones, pods or nuts either in groups or singly to the rope. Hang the finished garland with wires covered with large bows.

You can also make a garland in two parts for use over a doorway or mantle. When finished, this type of garland has the greens hanging down on each side.

An unusual shaped garland or festoon is often made of chicken wire (Fig. 7.3). Cut the wire to the desired length and then roll it into a cylinder. Next, flatten the cylinder

Fig. 7.3

into the shape for the finished festoon. Simply wire the materials directly to the chicken wire and hang, or use a Masonite or plywood background cut to shape and attach the chicken wire form to this.

A thin rope of greens is made in the same manner as a garland. However, with a rope, all the greens are wired facing the same direction.

Spray sweet gum tree balls or cones, thread them and hang as a rope on your Christmas tree.

WREATHS

COAT HANGER WREATH

Take a stout wire coat hanger (or fasten two together for strength) and bend it into a circular shape. Cut off the hook part. Cover the circle of wire with green florist's tape which not only disguises the wire but also prevents slippage of the greens.

Cut evergreens into 4 to 6-inch pieces. Take three or four sprays and wire the cut ends tightly together and then to the coat hanger frame. Aim the cut ends toward the direction that you plan to work. Wire a second bunch of sprays onto the framing, making certain that it overlaps the cut ends of the previous bunch wired on. Continue around the circle, wiring on greens until the frame is covered.

Attach wired cones or pods and tie on a bow to complete your coat hanger wreath. Juniper sprigs adorned with red sumac form the wreath in Figure 7.4.

As a variation of this design, you can mark off the middle of the top and the middle of the bottom of the coat hanger frame and wire the greens facing downward. For this, you start at the top center and wire the greens first on one side, increasing the size of the bunches as you progress down toward the bottom of the frame. Then start at the other side of the top and do likewise.

DOUBLE WIRE WREATH FRAME

The frame for a basic wreath consists of two circles made from heavy galvanized wire. The outer hoop is formed into a circle a bit smaller than the desired size wreath. The ends of the wire are overlapped by about 2 inches and wrapped securely with finer wire.

Form the second, inner circle in similar fashion, making it several inches smaller in diameter than the outer circle.

When the two circles are completed, cut several lengths of wire 3/4 inch longer than the width between the inner and outer circles. Form a hook on both ends of these wires with a pair of pliers and hook the two circles together. Slide the attached wires around the framework so that they are equally spaced. Secure these in place with finer wire or solder.

Cut cotton cloth (green or brown) or old sheeting dyed green into 1 1/2-inch strips. Attach one end of a strip onto the frame with a pin or a few stitches of thread.

Start winding a strip over the frame, making certain to overlap by about 1/2 inch and to have all the openings or pockets facing in the same direction. Don't pull the

Fig. 7.4

cloth too tightly, but then again, don't allow it to sag. These are the pockets for the greens, so you want ample room to insert stems and yet not too much room or they will drop out. When the entire frame is wrapped with cloth, sew the end of the strip in place.

Cut your greens into 4-inch pieces, inserting three to five stems into each pocket. Continue around the frame until all the pockets are filled.

Wire cones or other decorations directly onto the greens or onto florist's picks which are then inserted into the pockets. Add a big bow.

After the Christmas season, pull out the greens and save the frame.

Two double wire wreath frames are very effective when trimmed and used together as one. For instance, the pockets in a 16-inch frame are tucked with sprigs of white pine. Then the pockets in a wrapped 12-inch frame are stuffed with bits of yew. Wired cones, pods, nuts and berries adorn the 12-inch frame. Next, the two frames are wired together.

As a variation, perhaps the larger frame is wrapped with ribbon or velvet and only the smaller frame is trimmed with greens.

A flat double wire frame is frequently backed with 1/4-inch hardware cloth cut to the same shape and wired to the frame. Then greens, cones and other decorations are wired directly to the hardware cloth.

Styrofoam Wreath of Dried Materials

I prefer to use a 1 1/2-inch thick Styrofoam frame to which I glue a sturdy backing for added strength.

To begin, arrange your cones, pods and other dried materials of different shapes and sizes on your Styrofoam frame. When the design pleases you, remove a piece of dried material and make a nest by forming an indentation or by pulling out a bit of Styrofoam with a pair of tweezers. Squeeze Elmer's Glue-All into the depression and insert your material. Continue onto the next piece.

After all the larger dried materials are glued into place, glue tiny berries, cones or pieces of moss or lichen into any bare spaces. Add a bow or hang the wreath by a ribbon. The cone, pod, nut wreath shown in Figure 7.5 is sprayed gold.

Fig. 7.5

FLORIST'S WREATH

If you elect to use a florist's circular frame wreath (Fig. 7.6), pack the curve of the back with wet moss surrounded by green aluminum foil or green wax paper. Then tie the sealed "package" securely to the frame.

Cut evergreens into 4-inch pieces and push these into the moss "package" from the front of the frame. Wire the outside row first and then the inside row. A different kind of evergreen or a mixture of greens wired to the space between the other greens makes an interesting wreath.

If you use a florist's wreath frame for cones, dried materials or artificial greens, the moss "package" is not used. For a cone wreath, place the larger cones on the outer rim and the next in size on the inner rim of the frame. Wire the cones on the outer rim first, making certain that they are pulled tightly to the outer rim with their wires secured to the inner rim.

For the inner rim, tie the wires tightly on the cones, securing them to the outer rim. Between these two rows of cones, wire smaller cones, pods and nuts.

Fig. 7.6

NATIVITY SCENE AND STAR OF BETHLEHEM

NATIVITY SCENE

The simple nativity scene illustrated in Figure 7.7 is made of scrap cedar shakes. The base piece, 6 by 15 inches, received a single coat of green stain.

The side of the shelter is 2 by 4 inches and the roof is 2 by 8 inches. The outline of the back of the shelter is traced after the side and roof are nailed together. In this way, the shape of the back piece is cut so that a perfect fit is assured when nailed into place.

After you have made your shelter the size that you desire, snap off the scales from several medium-size pine cones with long-nosed pliers. Next, glue these on to the roof row by row with Elmer's Glue-All. Set aside to dry.

After the roof of the shelter dries, arrange the shelter on the base, set your figurines (plastic ones were used here) where you want them and add a few pine cones to represent trees. When pleased with the design, mark the base where the shelter and the trees are to stand.

Clear the base of materials and drill a small hole where each cone will stand. Now drill a shallow, small hole into each cone. (Two people are usually needed for this operation.) Next, spray your cones if you wish.

The next step is to hammer a nail into each hole from the bottom of the base. Add a drop of Duco Cement to each nail and slip on a cone. Finally, cement the shelter and the tiny figures in place.

Fig. 7.7

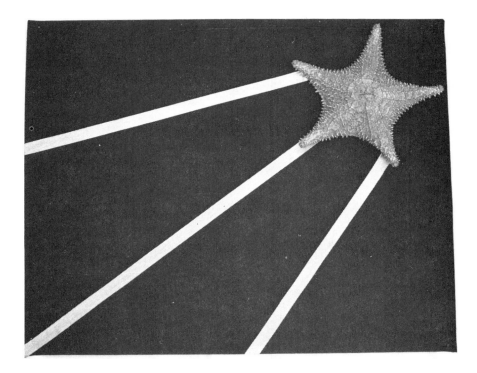

Fig. 7.8

STAR OF BETHLEHEM DOOR PLAQUE

Cut a piece of 1/8-inch Masonite approximately 32 inches wide by 28 inches high, or whatever size suitably fits your door.

Spray a giant sea star (the 10 to 12-inch size commonly sold in shops) with gold paint. When dry, attach several wires to the underside of the sea star. Next, position, but do not attach, the sea star on one of the upper corners of the Masonite, marking the places where the wires will pass through the Masonite. Now drill small holes where you have marked.

Cover the Masonite panel with dark blue cotton cloth, pulling it taut as you thumbtack the folded edges to the back of the Masonite.

Pass the wires attached to the sea star through the cloth and through the drilled holes. Pull the wires tight and twist them together in the back of the panel.

Use approximately 6 feet of 1 1/4-inch gold ribbon for the three rays radiating from the sea star. Position these and secure with Elmer's Glue-All. (Check the ribbon first with a bit of glue to make certain that it doesn't shrivel when glued.)

Four screws with star-shaped heads (one in each corner) will hold the sea star plaque sturdily in place on a door (Fig. 7.8).

A small wall plaque can also be made using the above idea. Secure a piece of blue felt to a piece of heavy cardboard or Masonite and glue on small sea stars and ribbons.

TREES AND ORNAMENTS

ORNAMENTS

There is an endless variety of Christmas ornaments which you can create with nature's collectibles. Here are just a few (see Fig. 7.9).

Spray a dried milkweed pod with two coats of gold paint. Glue a bit of preserved moss and a small artificial deer at the wider end of the pod. Make a tiny hole at the other end and thread a colorful ribbon or wire for hanging the ornament.

Spray sweet gum tree balls with gold. Wire them and they are ready to hang on your Christmas tree.

Cut out miniature cardboard wreaths and cover them on both sides with tiny cones, pods and seeds. Hang them onto the tree branches with bright ribbons.

TREES

LARGE CONE TREE

The large 14-inch sugar pine cone (see color insert) I collected in California makes an excellent miniature Christmas tree. This type cone is also sold in floral shops.

Drill a hole in the center of the bottom of the cone and then slip the hole over a long nail hammered into the bottom of a piece of wood. If the upright cone leans, use Stickum at the base to level it.

Miniature Christmas tree balls glued in place with Elmer's Glue-All adorn the cone scale branches.

SPIRAL CONE-SHAPED TOPIARY

A 9-inch-high Styrofoam cone is the base for the spiral cone-shaped topiary shown here (see color insert). (I used pearly everlastings, sweet gum tree balls and acorn cups with bits of moss added here and there.)

Begin your cone-shaped topiary by knotting two pieces of cord to a nail and pushing the nail into your cone at the very base. From this point, start spiraling the cords around until the peak is reached.

When you are satisfied with your cord spiral, glue one cord in place with Elmer's Glue-All and cut the other cord off. This extra cord is your tape measure. Stretch it out on your worktable and lay your cones, pods or other dried materials along its length. In this way, you will see just how many materials are needed for each spiral.

Starting at the base of the cone, one by one glue on the materials for the first spiral as close to the cord as possible. Use a tweezer to make a little nest or depression in the Styrofoam for each item and then squeeze glue into this pocket, adhering the materials closely together. When one spiral is finished, go on to the next.

Allow the cone to dry for 24 hours. Then fill in any tiny openings between the dried materials with a dab of glue applied with a toothpick and a small bit of preserved moss or lichen pressed into place with a pair of tweezers. Besides hiding any exposed Styrofoam, the moss or lichen adds color. Add an ornament to the top of the cone, if you so desire.

Fig. 7.9

A cone-shaped topiary can also be made by wrapping a piece of fan-shaped cardboard into the shape of a cone and then securing the two edges. Be sure to cut the backs of your materials so they are flat before gluing them in place on the cone.

RATTAN TREE

Rattan Christmas tree frames come in many sizes. The one in Figure 7.10 stands 24 inches high.

To start, spray the rattan frame gold or some other color. Then, wire small artificial candles to the frame in such a way as to form a pleasing design. (If you can't find the right size artificial candles, make them: use a small piece of cardboard to roll into candle form and then cover it with red craft paper, paint white drippings and a yellow cardboard flame.)

After the artificial candles are wired to the rattan form, surround the candles with sprigs of evergreen, wiring these to the frame, too.

Hang the candle tree flat against a wall or door.

HARDWARE CLOTH TREE

Using wire cutters, snip a triangle with 14-inch sides out of a piece of 1/4-inch hardware cloth. (Wear an old pair of gloves for this operation.) Next, cut out the straight sections of several flexible wire coat hangers. Weave these wires in and out around the edges of your hardware cloth triangle for strength.

Cut a triangle with 16-inch sides out of 1/8-inch Masonite. Position the hardware cloth frame on top of the cut Masonite, leaving an equal spacing of Masonite showing all around the edges of the hardware cloth. Now drill two holes 1/4 of an inch apart through the Masonite at the three angles of the hardware cloth. These holes are used later when joining the hardware cloth and Masonite.

Spray or paint the triangle of Masonite a desired shade of green. Set it aside to dry.

While the Masonite is drying, attach wired cones or pods to the hardware cloth frame. (Spruce cones are used in the design shown in Figure 7.11.) Slip the ends of the wire attached to each cone or pod through the framework and twist tightly in the back. Cut off the ends of the wires.

Cover the entire hardware cloth frame with dried materials. Proceed by wiring other pods or cones here and there as a second layer to give the design depth. In Figure 7.11, hemlock cones compose the second layer, with tiny red balls glued into position to give color to the natural-colored cones. When the frame design is completed, set it aside.

Cut a piece of 1-inch dowel, 12-inches long. This will be the trunk of the tree; about 5 inches supporting the tree in the back, 2 inches hidden in the container and the additional inches visible as the actual trunk. Now cut 5 inches of the dowel in half.

Screw the Masonite board to the halved dowel in two places with 1/2-inch screws.

Use a sturdy container, such as a 4 by 4 inch scrap of wood, sanded and painted. The one pictured is 2 1/4-inches high. Drill a 1-inch hole into the center of the wood to accept the dowel. If a pottery container filled with plaster of Paris is used, make certain that the completed tree won't be top heavy.

Fig. 7.10

Fig. 7.11

Hammer the dowel, with the Masonite board attached, into the container and then lay it down, positioning the completed hardware cloth design on top. Next, carefully loop a piece of wire at one corner of the hardware cloth and pass it through the two holes drilled in the Masonite. Twist the ends of the wire tightly together on the back of the Masonite. Secure the other two angles.

At this stage, pieces of either artificial evergreen or sprigs of natural greens are tucked around the edges, between the hardware cloth and the Masonite. When the holidays are over, all but the live greens are stored.

A tree shape or bell shape of cut hardware cloth can also be curved outward to give a three-dimensional effect for a wall or door hanging. A curved frame is covered with 3-inch sprigs of evergreen, cones or pods and then best attached to a heavy backing of wood or corrugated cardboard before it is hung. (Use only half a trunk or half a container for the tree so that it lies flat against any vertical surface.)

Adorn a hardware cloth bell with a colorful bow and hang a Christmas character on a length of ribbon the same color as the bow. Attach the ribbon within the bell and let the Christmas character hang down to serve as a bell clapper.

GEM TREE

Cut a small block of wood and drill a 1/4-inch hole halfway down into the center. Sand the block and either paint or stain it.

Cut a 4-inch piece of 1/4-inch dowel. Whittle one end to a point and then paint or stain the dowel.

When dry, press the pointed end of the dowel directly into the center of the base of a 3-1/2 inch Styrofoam cone. Push the dowel up into the cone for about 2 inches. Now holding the "tree" by the dowel, push the blunt end about 1/2 inch into the drilled hole in the wooden base.

Next, cover the upper part of the cone with white Stickum. Press tiny chips of polished gems into the Stickum, placing the gems closely together so as to conceal as much of the Stickum as possible. Progress downward on the cone, adding a bit of Stickum and then a few gem chips and so on until the form is completely covered (Fig. 7.12).

CENTERPIECES

CANDLE WREATH CENTERPIECE

To make a candle wreath centerpiece, start with a large 2-inch thick Styrofoam wreath form. When you decide on the number of candles you want to use on your wreath, mark off the place where each candle will stand and make a hole for the candle in the Styrofoam.

Poke the ends of short sprigs of juniper, taxus or arborvitae into the Styrofoam until the top and sides of the wreath form are covered. Decorate with tiny cones or pods sprayed with gold paint or left natural. Add little bows or Christmas balls for color; or place little deer or angels around your wreath.

Fig. 7.12

EVERGREEN CENTERPIECE

A large bowl of fresh fruit with touches of fresh evergreens tucked in here and there makes an appealing centerpiece. If a candle is used at each side of the bowl, surround each candle with bits of the same evergreen which you used in the bowl and add miniature artificial fruits to carry out your centerpiece design.

An evergreen swag that tapers on both ends creates an excellent basic design for an attractive centerpiece. Add fruits or cones or bows or Christmas tree balls to adorn the greens. Milkweed pod poinsettias (see index) or Queen Anne's lace "snowflakes" (see index) are other possibilities for dressing up your evergreen swag centerpiece.

CHRISTMAS BASKET

A small basket decorated in a Christmas motif serves as an interesting arrangement for an occasional table (Fig. 7.13).

Place small branches of live or artificial evergreens in the basket. Add cones, pods or other materials, either in their natural colors or sprayed. For a more appealing design, vary the shapes, sizes and textures of the materials. Place the most colorful, largest or most unusual materials in one section of the basket. This area, then, becomes the eye-catcher or focal point of your design.

The addition of a few colored Christmas tree balls is attractive. And, if you like, as a finishing touch, attach a bow to the basket.

Fig. 7.13

CANDLEHOLDERS

Cut a circle out of heavy cardboard or thin Masonite. Secure a large candle in the center of the circle with Stickum, melted wax or a sharp nail hammered from below.

Surround the candle with cones, pods and other dried materials, gluing them in place with Elmer's Glue-All as you proceed. Glue some of the materials over the first layer of cones and pods to give a three-dimensional effect. As you work out from the center, use smaller materials.

If desired, toward the outer rim of the circle, glue on some preserved moss to hide the cardboard edge and glue smaller cones and pods directly to this. Or if preferred, individual pine cone scales form a pleasing edging. For the finishing touches, add a few sprigs of artificial evergreen and some red berries (Fig. 7.14).

As a variation on this method, radiate five pine cones out from the candle. Glue in place and add greens and berries for color.

ADDITIONAL CHRISTMAS IDEAS AND GIFTS

IDEAS

The list of creative Christmas ideas is endless. Here are a few easy suggestions to help you get started.

Cut a large star out of 1/4-inch hardware cloth and cover it with evergreen clippings. Add a few colored materials and some padding to protect your door or wall and you are ready to hang your decoration.

Cut a semicircle out of plywood. Hammer 2-inch nails into the wood at regular intervals. Now wire evergreens, fruits, nuts, cones or pods to the nails. Hang over a mantle or doorway.

Pick dried-in-the-field Queen Anne's lace flower heads on short stems. Stand them in modeling clay and spray the stems and flower heads with gold or white paint. Add your white or golden "snowflakes" to window dressings or evergreen arrangements.

Spray snow or ice used on wreaths, windows, trees, mirrors and other holiday designs adds an extra dimension to your decor.

Cut a large heavy cardboard outline of a stocking. Take a large red or green stretch knee sock and insert the cardboard frame to give the stocking shape. Tuck greens, cones and colored balls in the top of the stocking and hang.

Cut a fan-shaped piece of 1/4-inch hardware cloth to whatever size you wish. Sew the two equal sides together with wire to form a cone. (Allow a 1/4-inch overlap.)

Stuff the cone with wads of paper held in place with crisscrossed wires. Cover the wires on the bottom of the cone by gluing felt into place.

Glue a suitable dowel into a drilled hole in a wooden base or use plaster of Paris to secure the dowel in a container. Push the other (pointed) end of the dowel through the stuffing in the cone up to the peak.

Wire dried materials to small floral picks, dip the wooden tips into glue and insert into the hardware cloth cone. When the cloth cone is covered, fill the interspaces with bits of moss, lichens or tiny flowers.

Fig. 7.14

This same idea can be used with live evergreens by filling the cone with damp moss in place of the paper.

Spray an interestingly shaped branch with white, gold or silver paint. While still wet, add bits of glitter. Mount the branch in a container of clay, Styrofoam or plaster of Paris. Decorate the branch with colored Christmas tree balls, dried flowers, cones, pods or tiny artificial birds.

The tiny cones from alder trees make perfect miniature Christmas trees for mini-scenes.

Wire or glue pine cones to a cardboard cone. Start at the base and gradually work around the cone until it is totally covered with pine cones. Top the peak of the cone with an upright pine cone. Spray the cone tree if you like.

Glue a cone star (Fig. 7.15) to the center of a plastic shortening or coffee can top. Attach a wire through the top so that it may be hung from the back. Glue artificial greens and berries around the star for color. Hang as a wall or window ornament.

Milkweed Pod Poinsettia

Thread five dried milkweed pods onto florist's wire. Run the wire through the wide ends of the pods and then pull the ends of the wire together until the pods radiate out from the wire in a circle (Fig. 7.16). Next, twist the ends of the wire together and cut off any excess wire.

With spray paint, coat both sides of your "star-flower" with red enamel. Since the dried pods are very absorbent, two coats of enamel are usually necessary.

When the enameled flower is dry, cut yellow wool or yellow pipe cleaners into varying lengths from 1/2 to 1 1/4 inches. Glue these into the center of the flower, tipping a few of them with white enamel.

Use these milkweed pod poinsettias combined with greens for centerpieces or door designs.

Ham Can Christmas Decoration

For this project, you will need the container from a canned ham. Any size will do, since the size of the can you use merely determines the size of your completed project. I used the can from a 3-pound ham (Fig. 7.17).

Important: The can is not opened in the conventional way, using the key attached to the can. Instead, both sides of the can are opened with a can opener.

Next, wash the can thoroughly with detergent and water. When the can dries, sand any sharp edges on the metal.

The ham can is now ready for decorating. The two outer sides of the can (Fig. 7.17) are decorated with small hemlock cones, but you can use any small pods or cones.

Use the top seam of the ham can as a center line and begin by cementing (Duco) your cones or other materials a little to one side of this line. Proceed row by row across the side of the can, using old rags to prop up the can so that the cemented cones won't slip off the metal before they adhere.

After one side of the can is covered with your decorative materials, allow it to dry for 24 hours before covering the remaining surface.

Next, spray the dried materials on the can with several coats of gold paint, making certain that all the materials and the outer surfaces of the can are covered.

The next step is lining the inside of the ham can with ribbon, felt, velvet or with whatever material desired. If you use a fabric, test a piece before gluing it into place and make certain that you use a glue that adheres to metal.

Fig. 7.15

Fig. 7.16

Once the lining of the can is dry, there are endless uses for your new ornament. Perhaps a bit of evergreen secured with modeling clay might set the scene for a lovely madonna or a ball-shaped topiary.

Three decorated ham cans of different sizes adorned with Christmas greens and figures create a charming mantle or sideboard arrangement.

CHRISTMAS FAVORS

To make a pine cone Santa (Fig. 7.18), attach the flat end of a large pine cone to a small piece of wood or cardboard. Trim the scales on the pointed end of the cone until it is flat. Now flatten the pointed end of a smaller cone of the same kind. Cement the two blunt ends of the cones together. Cement two artificial plastic eyes and a red artificial holly berry for a nose. White cotton hair and a beard are cemented in place next. Cut a simple red cap of felt, cementing a small ball of white cotton to its peak. Glue Santa's cap in place.

To make a miniature winter scene, spray part of a small pocket mirror with artificial snow. Add a few tiny sprigs of evergreen and a small plastic deer. Or, cement a few small upright pine cones onto the mirror and spray the entire scene with snow.

Pine cones of all sizes make interesting miniature trees. You can stand small cones on wood or in tiny containers, using modeling clay or Stickum to hold them upright. Spray them with clear acrylic or gold and, while wet, sprinkle with sequins or colored glitter. Cover the base surrounding a standing pine cone tree with cotton or spray snow to complete the winter scene. Also, add bits of cotton or snow to the tips of the cone.

KISSING BALLS

A kissing ball is a sphere covered with flowers, fruits, evergreens or other foliage from which a few sprigs of mistletoe hang suspended.

Spray a large Styrofoam ball with green Styrofoam paint, if the ball is white, or cover a white ball by gluing preserved moss securely in place.

With a pencil, pierce the Styrofoam ball directly through the center. Pull an inexpensive gold chain or a ribbon through the hole until about 4 inches of chain or ribbon extend past the ball. Knot the top end of the chain or ribbon so that it can't be pulled through the hole. This is the underside of the kissing ball.

Allow 8 to 10 inches of chain or ribbon to extend out of the upper side of the ball for hanging purposes.

Cut 3-inch sprigs of artificial evergreen or other foliage and stick the ends of these into the ball as close together as you can. Add miniature artificial fruits or other colorful materials.

When the ball is completely covered, add a small spray of mistletoe and a bow to the lower end of the chain or ribbon. (Mistletoe berries are extremely poisonous if eaten, so use artificial mistletoe if there are young children in the home.)

Hang your kissing ball in a doorway or attach it to a ceiling fixture in your entrance hall or foyer (Fig. 7.19).

Note: a big round potato, used in place of the Styrofoam ball, makes an excellent base for keeping live greens fresh.

Fig. 7.17

Fig. 7.18

CHRISTMAS CARDS

First press some leaves or single layers of evergreen sprigs (sliced thin with a sharp razor blade) in a telephone book. Weight the book for about a week.

Next, glue a pressed leaf or piece of evergreen to a small block of wood. Press this form against a colored ink pad and then onto your stationery.

As an alternative method, place a pressed leaf or piece of evergreen on a folded sheet of stationery. Gently spray a mist of paint over the foliage and the paper until the paper is peppered with paint, except for under the greens. When you remove the foliage, the outline remains. (See Chapter 4 for other ideas.)

Fig. 7.19

GIFTS

Along with the festive decor we associate with the holiday season, Christmas is traditionally a gift-giving time of year. Friends and relatives appreciate the thoughtfulness of a handmade gift. The animal world presents numerous gift ideas and designs, in addition to the nature crafts discussed throughout this book. Here are a few gifts created from the world of animals.

ANIMAL TRACK CASTS

To get really interesting animal tracks, take a hike into the woods, especially along a stream bed. Pack a knapsack with the supplies that you will need—plaster of Paris, a small plastic pail (easy to clean because dried plaster pops out), a canteen of water, several thin cardboard strips cut to approximately 2 by 18 inches, paper clips, a stirring stick and rags.

First find a clear animal track in mud or firm wet sand. If there are any leaves or other loose debris in the imprint, remove them.

Take one of your thin, precut cardboard strips and curve it to form a ring large enough to encircle the track. Use a paper clip to hold the circle the size you want. Carefully press the cardboard circle into the ground around the track.

Read the directions on your bag of plaster of Paris very carefully. Pour the correct amount of water into the plastic pail. Now add the plaster of Paris to the water very slowly, stirring it constantly until it is the consistency of thin pudding.

Next, hold the pail over the cardboard form and allow the plaster of Paris mixture to flow into the animal track, making certain that the deepest part of the track is filled first. Fill the cardboard circle to about 1/4 inch from the top and then smooth the surface of the plaster with the stick.

Allow anywhere from 1/2 to 1 hour for the plaster to dry. (If you wish to insert a picture wire for later hanging, do so before the plaster sets solidly.) Before picking up your cast, test the plaster for hardness. If you cannot press your fingerprints into the center of the plaster, it has hardened enough to handle.

To remove your plaster animal track, carefully free the ground around it and gently pull the cast up from the ground. Remove the collar and place the cast in a rag and tuck it into your pack.

At home, thoroughly wash the plaster of Paris form to remove all the earth and sand. Use a toothbrush to remove stubborn earth. This is now your negative print.

To make the positive animal print (the way you see the animal depression in nature), first coat the surface of the negative with a thin layer of Vaseline. Then use a rubber band to hold a 4-inch-wide strip of cardboard around the cast.

Again prepare a plaster of Paris mixture and pour it into the cardboard collar. The mixture should be poured so that it covers the highest point on the negative by at least 3/4 inch. Smooth the surface of the plaster with the stirring stick and then set the cast aside for about an hour to dry. If you so desire, insert a picture wire during the drying process for hanging.

When the plaster of Paris is dry, separate the two pieces. Your second casting is the positive print. Sand any rough surfaces on the sides or bottoms of the casts.

If you like, for protection, coat the casts with shellac or varnish; or paint the surfaces a ground color with a slightly darker shade on the imprint or on the raised part of the cast; or brush a light coating of Elmer's Glue-All onto the casts and sprinkle on some fine sand.

If you cut a piece of felt and glue it to the base, your animal track casts will make unusual and interesting paperweights.

RUBBER STAMP FOOTPRINTS

Start by tracing or sketching several animal footprints. (Borrow books with animal tracks from your local library.) Make life-size drawings of several tracks on cardboard and cut them out.

Cut an old inner tube into large flat sections. Place a cardboard cutout onto a piece of inner tube and outline it with a sharp pencil. Then cut out the rubber outline with sharp scissors or tin snips. Reverse your cardboard cutout, pencil onto another piece of rubber and cut it out. You now have a pair of footprints.

Use Duco to cement the footprints to a small block of wood. Weight the rubber footprints down to dry.

Rubber stamp footprints can be inked on a stamp pad or with a brayer. Place several sheets of newspaper underneath the paper that you are stamping to give a cushioning effect; this will give you a clearer print.

Purchase a tube of black or waterproof paint at an art shop. Squeeze a dab of the paint onto a scrap piece of glass. Roll the paint out with the brayer. Next, roll your paint-coated brayer over your rubber footprints.

At first, experiment by stamping old sheeting and rags. Then try stamping footprints onto fabrics or towels for unique and personalized gifts.

FAKE FUR WALL HANGING

To start, determine the size of the fake fur wall hanging that you plan on making. The one shown in Figure 7.20 measures 62 by 44 inches. Then select the fake fur yardage needed. (Use 54-inch wide fabric.)

Next, draw a simple animal outline on a piece of paper and expand your drawing to the desired size on a large piece of brown wrapping paper which is folded lengthwise.

When satisfied with your large paper outline, buy a piece of 1/4-inch plywood of the size needed for your particular project. (Plywood is difficult to obtain in sheets more than 4 feet wide, so don't think too big!)

Lay your large sheet of plywood on the floor. With a pencil, trace the opened outline onto the plywood. Then cut the plywood with a keyhole saw or a power sabre saw.

Lay the fabric flat (wrong side up) onto the floor. Then place the plywood framework in the center, making certain that the back stripe, if the fake fur has one, lies in the center of the wooden framework.

To attach the fake fur, pull it taut a small section at a time, cutting off the excess material as you go along except for about 2 inches which you use to staple (with a staple

Fig. 7.20

gun) to the back of the framework. Make certain that you always keep your fabric taut as you work, otherwise the fake fur will sag in places when hung.

Suspend your completed fake fur wall hanging by wires attached to the back or by nails. Hang it at a definite slant.

You may also want to cover foam rubber pillow forms to match.

FAKE FUR BOXES

Buy an inexpensive wooden box with a recessed top. Cut a piece of fake fur to fit the recess.

Brush a coating of Elmer's Glue-All onto the recess of the box and press the fake fur into place (Fig. 7.21).

To cover a simple rectangular or square-shaped wooden box with fake fur, first measure the height of the bottom half of the box. Then measure the total perimeter of the four sides of the box.

Cut a long strip of fake fur the width and the perimeter (four sides) of the base of the box. Glue this strip around the four sides with Elmer's Glue-All. Set aside.

Place a piece of fake fur wrong side up on your worktable. Lay the box cover (inside up) on the fur. Now mark with a pencil where the four sides of the box cover will reach on the fur. Cut the piece of fake fur roughly to the size of the cover and its sides.

Remove the box cover and coat the top with Elmer's Glue-All. Position the cover on the center of the fur and weight it down to dry.

When the top of the cover dries, fold two parallel sides of the fake fur down onto the sides of the cover. With scissors, trim to the proper width and then glue these sides in place. Use snap clothespins to apply pressure while the glue is drying.

To continue, make a cut at each end of the glued sides (where the fur doesn't touch the side of the box). Now glue the two remaining sides into place.

To finish your box cover (when the sides are dry), very carefully cut off the four flaps of fur which extend out from each corner of the cover. Apply a dab of glue to each corner, if necessary, to make a tight bond where the edges of the fake fur meet (Fig. 7.21).

Fig. 7.21

Chapter *8*
Decorations
for Other Holidays
and Party Favors

Throughout the year, nature's collectibles add interest and charm to our holiday and party decorations.

VALENTINE'S DAY HEARTS

First, decide on the size of the heart design you want to make. Naturally, a centerpiece heart will be larger than one to grace a dresser or an end table.

Purchase a piece of flat, 1-inch thick Styrofoam. Sketch a heart shape on the Styrofoam and then cut it out with a knife. (Make an open center design if you like.)

Next, cut tiny sprigs of preserved baby's breath or statice (either from your collection or purchased) and press the ends of the stems into the Styrofoam. When the sides and the surface are covered, add miniature red roses or rose buds (either those preserved in a desiccant or tiny natural-looking artificial ones).

EASTER EGGS

To start, select a white or brown egg. The first step is to blow the egg out of its shell. A room-temperature egg is easier to work with but it's not impossible to blow an egg which just came from the refrigerator. Just blow a little harder to get the contents out. (I save eggshells over a period of time, simply blowing an egg each time I need one.)

To blow an egg, first make a tiny hole in one end of the eggshell with a needle, pin or the tip of a skewer. Then, make a slightly larger hole in the opposite end.

Pierce the egg yolk and stir around in the shell with the pointed object. Next, take a big breath, press your mouth over the smaller hole and, holding the egg over a bowl, blow. The contents of the egg will come sputtering out of the larger hole.

When all the contents are removed, place the larger hole of the egg under the faucet and allow a little water to flow into the egg. Shake the egg and blow the water out.

Save empty egg cartons for drying and storing eggs.

To decorate a blown egg, use Elmer's Glue-All to affix pressed flowers, ferns or leaves to the shell, using the wide end of the egg as the bottom. To dry, run one end of a stiff wire through the larger hole of the egg, allowing the end of the wire to rest on the inside shell at the opposite end. Stand the other end of the wire in modeling clay. When the glue dries, spray the entire egg with several coats of clear acrylic.

When the acrylic spray dries, slide the egg off the wire. If the egg is to be hung, glue a 1/4-inch decorative, gold braid lengthwise around the egg, making certain that it covers the two holes on the ends. At the pointed end of the egg, insert and glue a 4-inch length of gold cord under the braid. Knot the ends of the cord for hanging.

Spray an interestingly shaped branch with white, gold or pastel paint. Insert the base of the branch into a container of stones or plaster of Paris. Hang your decorated eggs onto the tips of the branches. The eggs on the tree shown in Figure 8.1 are adorned with pressed scilla, ferns, forsythia, pansy and Queen Anne's lace.

If the decorated eggs aren't to be used for hanging, then cover the end holes in the eggs with the pressed flower materials. Use these eggs in baskets or as party favors.

FALL-WINTER DECOR

BASKET ARRANGEMENTS

A basket of any size can be used for a fall-winter arrangement. A small basket might be placed on a table or a shelf while a larger basket could be set on the floor in a foyer, hall or near a fireplace.

Make an arrangement in your basket with the berries, cones, pods and other dried materials which you collect in the fall. During the December holiday season, put the basket away for a few weeks. After New Year's Day, when you've packed away your Christmas decorations, bring your basket arrangement out again and enjoy it until spring arrives.

My fall-winter basket (see color insert) contains bayberries, bittersweet berries, acorn cups, evergreen cones of several kinds, sweet gum tree balls, sumac berry spike, locust pods, halved Princess-tree pods, chartreuse lichens, milfoil, evening primrose stalks, goldenrod skeletons and bracket fungus. A small artificial bird is perched on the milfoil.

When you make your fall-winter basket, carefully select the materials to be used. Different shapes, textures, sizes and harmonious colors are the necessary ingredients for visual enjoyment.

ORNAMENTAL GOURDS

If you grow your own gourds, harvest them in the late summer when their stems turn brown and dry. This is the sign that the gourds are ripe. Leave any unripe gourds on the vines until the first frost is expected. Then, using a sharp knife or pruning shears, cut the stems of the gourds. Leave a few inches of stem on each gourd.

To clean home-grown or untreated, purchased gourds, first wash them in warm, sudsy water. Then rinse the gourds in a mixture of disinfectant and water to clean the

surfaces thoroughly from dirt and bacteria. Pat each gourd dry with a soft towel so as not to damage the shell.

To dry gourds thoroughly, space them on a piece of plastic or aluminum screening which is propped up (or tacked to wood) to allow complete air circulation around them. Place this drying rack in a warm, dry place.

After about 10 days, the skin of the gourds begins to harden. Immature gourds soften and should be thrown away.

Next, wipe each hardened gourd with a soft rag dipped in disinfectant. Wipe the screening on the drying rack with disinfectant, too. Again space the gourds on the screening and place in a dry, warm, dark place for about a month to preserve as much of the natural color of the gourds as possible.

After your gourds are dried, you may want to wax them or give them a coat of shellac or even paint. However, they may be used just as they are from the drying rack.

Use your preserved gourds in fall baskets with strawflowers, bittersweet or other dried materials. Wooden bowls, rattan cornucopias and trays are other suitable containers for gourd arrangements.

DOOR DESIGNS

In the fall, tie three ears of decorative corn together by their husks. Hang on your front door as traditional sign of welcome.

If you wish, start with three ears of decorative corn and tie on other dried materials such as plant spikes, leaves, nuts, stalks of grain and other fall treasures until you have created a fall swag for your door. All dried materials to be used outdoors should first be sprayed with clear acrylic spray.

Creating a fall-winter door plaque is a special endeavor.

To start, select a piece of sturdy wood and saw it into a panel the size you desire. The weathered cedar shake illustrated in Figure 8.2 measures 19 by 6 1/2 inches.

Choose the dried materials from your storage boxes which you plan to use on your door panel. Arrange the materials on the panel until you get the desired effect. Then, one by one, use Duco Cement to affix each piece. Use different sizes, textures and pleasing colors to create your design.

Attach your plaque to a door with nails or screws at the top and bottom.

The panel in Figure 8.2 consists of chartreuse lichens, sumac berry spike, flicker feathers, horse's hoof fungus, pine cones, mahogany fungus, hemlock cones, tulip-tree seeds and sweet gum tree balls.

HALLOWEEN DECORATIONS

For Halloween, buy a large pumpkin and decorate it with a carrot for a nose, carrot tops (or other greens) for hair, sliced radishes for eyes, green peppers (halved) for ears and string beans for a mouth. Attach the adornments either by cutting away a bit of the pumpkin's shell to insert and then glue them or by using straight pins to hold them in place.

Carve a pumpkin with a sharp knife. First carve the top by slanting the knife into the

Fig. 8.2

pumpkin so that the cut top will be larger than the hole. Next, use a large metal stirring spoon to scrape out all the seeds and stringy pulp.

With a pencil, lightly sketch two triangular-shaped eyes, a triangular-shaped nose and a smiling partly toothed mouth. When pleased with the location of the features, slant the knife so that it cuts the inside larger than the outside. Push in the cut pieces with your fingers and remove them through the hole in the top.

Fill your pumpkin with large sprays of dried materials to make a Halloween pumpkin arrangement. Or, do the usual by attaching a candle inside so that the pumpkin can be lit up.

THANKSGIVING DESIGNS

Buy an inexpensive cornucopia basket. Fill it with fresh fruits, nuts, gourds and stalks of grain. Let the materials used spill out onto the table. Use as a centerpiece for a table or on the kitchen counter.

Purchase a large pineapple with the long spiny leaves intact. Decorate the pineapple to look like a turkey and use as a centerpiece on the Thanksgiving Day table.

To make a pineapple turkey, first cut two pieces of red felt to measure approximately 7 1/2 by 2 1/2 inches. Trim these pieces of felt to resemble the head and neck of the turkey (Fig. 8.3). Cut a wavy length of red felt approximately 6 inches long and 1/2 inch wide to represent the wattle.

Either by hand or on a sewing machine, sew the two head and neck pieces together (leave the base open). Insert the end of the wattle as you sew near the bill area. (Pink the edges of the felt on the head and neck if you like.) Stuff the head and neck with cotton and add a stiff wire or skewer for attaching to a pineapple. Glue a plastic eye or a sequin to each side of the head; glue a notched orange felt triangle for a bill.

Use the wire or skewer to secure the turkey's head and neck to the bottom edge of a large pineapple which is lying flat. The leaves of the pineapple serve as a tail.

If you like, add colorful tail feathers by cutting a semicircle of yellow felt. Scallop the edges. Then cut several oval orange, brown and green felt feathers and glue these with Elmer's Glue-All to the semicircle. Use straight pins to attach the yellow felt so that it looks like a large fan-shaped tail.

APPLE PYRAMIDS

The size of the framework to create an apple pyramid is determined by the size of the apples to be used in the design. Decide on the size of the fruit before you start and on whether to use real or artificial apples.

The apple pyramid in Figure 8.4 is made of inexpensive artificial fruit. Each apple is approximately 1 3/4 inches long and the pineapple stands 5 inches high. The framework is a wooden cone 5 1/2 inches high and was made from a cone-shaped piece of decorative wood.

To start your apple pyramid, select a wooden base and a cone-shaped piece of wood or a log. From the bottom of the base, hammer in several inch-long nails to hold the wooden framework upright. Surround the base of the upright framework with Stickum for added sturdiness.

Next, remove the stems from the apples and surround the upright framework with the apples. (The bottom row on the pyramid pictured contains seven small apples.) After you have the apples arranged around the base of the upright framework, mark and then drill a hole slanted downward where the center of each apple is located. Now use Duco Cement to affix a nail (or skewer) of the proper length into each hole. Allow the Duco to dry for several hours.

Continue your pyramid by inserting the bottom row of apples onto the nails. Now stagger the next row of apples (six in the picture) and drill holes for their centers. Cement the nails in place and allow to dry. Insert the centers of the second row of apples onto the nails. Stagger the top tier of apples (four in the pictured pyramid). Drill holes, cement in nails and allow to dry. Then insert this final row of apples.

To top an artificial apple pyramid, cut a hole in the base of the artificial pineapple and slip it over the tip of the cone. Use Stickum to hold the pineapple in place. Insert

Fig. 8.3

Fig. 8.4

apple leaves or other plastic greens between the apples. Use Stickum to hold the greens in place.

If making a real apple pyramid, cut the top of the cone flat and set a real pineapple in place. Fill the openings between the apples with greens of your choice.

PARTY FAVORS

ACORN PEOPLE

To make the acorn boy illustrated in Figure 8.5, use two large, cleaned baked acorns and one large acorn cup.

For the head, draw eyes, nose, mouth and hair on one of the acorns with a black, waterproof felt-tipped pen. (Position the flat bottom of the acorn toward the neck.)

With an ice pick, make a hole at the flat end of the body acorn. Make two armholes on the side of the body acorn and two holes near the tip of the body acorn for the legs.

Cut five short lengths of pipe cleaners. Insert and cement these for the arms, legs and as a connecting link between the head and body. Bend the tips of the two legs to form feet.

Fig. 8.5

Cement the acorn cup (hat) onto the head and cement the feet to a piece of wood or cardboard. Cut tiny mittens out of construction paper or felt and cement these to the pipe cleaner hands. Tie a colorful little piece of wool around the neck as a scarf.

ACORN CUP FAVORS

Wash and dry an acorn cup. Sand the bottom of the cup so that it sits level. Cement preserved moss into the cup and cement a preserved or artificial mushroom to the moss (Fig. 8.5).

As a variation, pat Stickum into the bottom of an acorn cup and insert tiny stems of dried plant materials. Hide the Stickum with preserved moss, pebbles or tiny chips of polished gems. Tiny pieces of dock and miniature strawflowers adorn the acorn cup (Fig. 8.5).

MILKWEED POD FAVORS

Wash and dry an open milkweed pod. Coat both sides of the pod with clear acrylic spray. Cement a bit of moss to the bottom of the pod; cement dried plant materials onto the moss. Cemented to the pod in Figure 8.5 are a tiny mushroom, hemlock cone, lichen and an acorn in its cup.

You can also fill a clean, opened milkweed pod (or half a walnut shell or seashell) with tiny candies or nuts.

PINE CONE TURKEY FAVOR

Select a large pine cone with a flat bottom. Use the cone on its side for your turkey.

Cut two fan-shaped pieces of felt (one larger than the other) to serve as the tail feathers. Cut notches on each piece of felt so that it resembles feathers. In Figure 8.6, orange and tan felt was used.

Cement the larger tail piece in place between the rows of scales near the pointed end of the cone. Cement the smaller tail piece a few rows closer to the head.

Cut a piece of red felt to serve as the turkey's head and neck. Cut this double and then fold it around a stiff piece of wire. Cement the felt neck and head to the wire. Use the pressure of a snap clothespin when drying the neck and head.

Cut a double piece of orange felt for the turkey's bill. Cement in place; cement two plastic or button eyes using the snap clothespin to apply pressure.

Push the end of the neck and wire in between the scales at the front of the turkey's body. Cement in place.

Finally, bend two halves of orange pipe cleaners for the legs and feet. Cement in place.

PINE CONE OWL FAVORS

Select two clean, dry pine cones with flat bottoms. One cone should be slightly larger than the other.

Lay the larger cone (for the body) on its side on your worktable. Now use pliers to pinch off part of the outer scales where the cone touches your table. Cut a little and then

Fig. 8.6

test until the cone stands on this flattened side without rocking. Save two of the cut scales for ear tufts.

When the one side of the large cone is flattened, set it with the natural flat bottom facing you. Take the smaller cone (for the head) also with the flat bottom facing you and press its scales into the scales on the body cone. When the scales interlock, squeeze a few drops of cement between the scales to hold the cones permanently in place.

Cement the two scales, which you saved, in place for ear tufts. Cement two plastic or button eyes to the owl. Then cut a narrow orange triangle out of felt and cement on for a beak.

Use your owl as a Halloween favor; or cement it or an entire family of owls to a branch of decorative wood (Fig. 8.7).

Create your own party favors using a pine cone for the body of a person, bird or other animal. Use an acorn or a tiny Styrofoam ball for the head. Draw eyes, nose, and mouth or use sequins or beads instead. Use pipe cleaners for arms, legs and a neck. Bend the feet so that the person or animal either stands or sits by itself or is glued to a small piece of wood (Fig. 8.8).

Fig. 8.7

Fig. 8.8

MIRROR FAVORS

To make an elegant party favor, start with a pocket mirror purchased in a dime store.

Set the mirror on your worktable and place a tiny mound of Stickum toward one end of the mirror. Press dried plant materials into the Stickum. Cover the Stickum with pebbles, gem chips or preserved moss.

You can also make a miniature plant party favor like the bittersweet sprig shown in Figure 8.9. Insert the sprig in a small container of clay and affix to a mirror or a small piece of wood.

Fig. 8.9

PLACE CARD HOLDERS

Place card holders can be made of thin scrap wood, thick cardboard covered with fabric or scrap paneling.

Cut each place card holder approximately 3 by 1 1/4 inches. This size allows for a small decoration as well as a name card.

Decorate one section of each place card holder. Cement on tiny shells, cones and pods or dried flowers (Fig. 8.10).

When the decorations dry, cut a small strip of colored paper to fit into the undecorated part of the place card holder. Print the guest's name on the paper in colored ink. Press the paper in place on the holder with a tiny bit of Stickum.

After the party is over, you can pull off the colored papers and save the place card holders or give them away as party favors.

Fig. 8.10

Index

(Items in **bold** refer to illustrations)

Anne
Orth
Epple

A native of Tuckahoe, New York, I was raised in an atmosphere of nature. My mother's enthusiasm for flowering plants soon became a vital part of my childhood. At this same time, my older brother's intense interest in animals also greatly influenced me. Before I reached the age of ten, I knew that in some way my vocation would touch on my interest in nature.

When I was old enough to serve as a camp counselor, I spent several summers teaching nature to campers in the New York area. Then, the summer after high school graduation, I served for two months as co-director at a summer museum where I taught children about plants and animals, as well as cared for the animals on display in the museum. That summer's rich experience led directly to six exciting years as "Zoo Lady" of the Bronx Zoo. Using animals from the zoo, I lectured at schools, institutions and to other interested groups.

Now as a busy mother and homemaker, nature still dominates much of my life. Free moments are spent creating crafts from nature's many collectibles; writing magazine articles and children's and craft books on nature; caring for animals in need; and gardening. Fortunately, my husband and sons share my love for the out-of-doors and enjoy backpacking and camping which takes each of us closer to nature.